Buddha Takes the Mound

ALSO BY DONALD LOPEZ JR.

Seeing the Sacred in Samsara

Gendun Chopel: Tibet's Modern Visionary

Hyecho's Journey: The World of Buddhism

Dispelling the Darkness: A Jesuit's Quest for the Soul of Tibet

The Lotus Sūtra: A Biography

Strange Tales of an Oriental Idol

From Stone to Flesh: A Short History of the Buddha

Buddhism: The Norton Anthology of World Religions

The Scientific Buddha: His Short and Happy Life

The Tibetan Book of the Dead: A Biography

Buddhism and Science: A Guide for the Perplexed

The Madman's Middle Way

Critical Terms for the Study of Buddhism

The Story of Buddhism

A Modern Buddhist Bible

Prisoners of Shangri-La: Tibetan Buddhism and the West

Elaborations on Emptiness: Uses of the Heart Sūtra

Curators of the Buddha: The Study of Buddhism Under Colonialism

The Princeton Dictionary of Buddhism

Buddha Takes the Mound

ENLIGHTENMENT IN 9 INNINGS

DONALD LOPEZ JR.

ST. MARTIN'S
ESSENTIALS
NEW YORK

First published in the United States by St. Martin's Essentials,
an imprint of St. Martin's Publishing Group

www.stmartins.com

Designed by Steven Seighman

Library of Congress Cataloging-in-Publication Data

Names: Lopez, Donald S., Jr., 1952– author.
Title: Buddha takes the mound : enlightenment in nine innings /
  Donald S. Lopez Jr.
Description: First edition. | New York : St. Martin's Essentials, 2020
Identifiers: LCCN 2019051874 | ISBN 9781250237910 (paper over board) |
  ISBN 9781250237927 (ebook)
Subjects: LCSH: Baseball—Religious aspects—Buddhism.
Classification: LCC GV867 .L67 2020 | DDC 796.357072/7—dc23
LC record available at https://lccn.loc.gov/2019051874

Our books may be purchased in bulk for promotional, educational,
or business use. Please contact your local bookseller or the Macmillan
Corporate and Premium Sales Department at 1-800-221-7945, extension
5442, or by email at MacmillanSpecialMarkets@macmillan.com.

First Edition: May 2020

10 9 8 7 6 5 4 3 2 1

CONTENTS

PREFACE I

ESTABLISHING THE BONA FIDES 3

THE BASEBALL SUTRA, WITH COMMENTARY

1. THE PROLOGUE 21

2. THE QUESTION 29

3. IMPERMANENCE 46

4. SUFFERING 61

5. NO SELF 73

6. KARMA 90

7. VAJRAPANI 104

8. THE SECRET TEACHING 116

9. ENLIGHTENMENT 132

APPENDIX: THE BASEBALL SUTRA 145

PREFACE

The first of the Buddha's famous four noble truths is "All is suffering." More than any other sport, baseball is suffused with suffering. The best batters fail to get a hit 70 percent of the time. The scoreboard in every stadium each day displays a giant E (for errors). Relief pitchers are judged not by their wins but by their saves, the number of times they avert disaster. A team that loses four of every ten games always goes to the playoffs; a team that loses five of every ten games never does. The season seems endless—162 games—many endured in "the dog days of August."

This book demonstrates that baseball is a Buddhist game. Like Buddhism, baseball has its own elaborate universe, with good karma leading to rebirth as a god in the major leagues, an abode of private planes and luxury suites. Bad karma leads to rebirth in one of the trifling hells of the minor leagues, with names like "Low A," with smelly buses and cheap motels. Over the course of a career, a player wanders between these worlds. Only a tiny few ascend to nirvana, located in Cooperstown, New York, where the relics of the saints are enshrined: the bat, the ball, the glove, the cap, the cleats—just as the Buddha's relics are enshrined in pagodas.

Baseball has often been called a religion, with places like Fenway Park and Wrigley Field regularly referred to as "shrines." (The word "fan" is derived from "fanatic.") This book demonstrates that that religion is Buddhism, where life is described as an endless round of suffering, from one lifetime to the next, marked by inevitable yet unpredictable loss. We suffer this loss each season, futilely hoping that the next lifetime—the next season—might be different. And yet the promise of enlightenment awaits.

ESTABLISHING THE BONA FIDES

I am a Yankees fan. I was born on June 1, 1952. The Yankees did not play. The next day they beat the Indians 2-0 at Yankee Stadium, a four-hit complete game shutout by Allie Reynolds. Mickey Mantle, leading off and playing right field, went 1 for 4, a double off Bob Lemon, who was 22-11 that year. My first memory of a Yankees game was when I was eight years old, Game Seven of the 1960 World Series, when the Pirates' second baseman Bill Mazeroski (who had hit eleven home runs that season) hit a walk-off home run off Ralph Terry (who had given up fifteen home runs in 166.2 innings that season). Yogi Berra was playing left field that day, and I still remember him running back and then reversing course and turning toward the dugout as the ball went over the high ivied walls of Forbes Field. This memory is in black and white, the colors on the television screen, the colors of the Pirates' uniforms.

The other defining moment of my devotion to the Yankees was Game Seven of the 2001 World Series, when Mariano Rivera broke the bat of Luis Gonzalez, producing a bloop over a drawn-in infield. The ball landed exactly where Derek Jeter would have been standing had he been playing at normal depth. Or that's what I read. I turned off the television before the ball hit the ground. That memory is in an offensive shade of teal, the color of the Diamondbacks' uniforms. I have never watched a replay of that game, or a clip of that "hit." It's too painful.

Over those forty-two years, from 1960 to 2001, the Yankees won the pennant fourteen times and won the World Series eight times, more than any other team. I remember all of those titles: Willie McCovey hitting a screamer right at Bobby Richardson in Candlestick Park, Game Seven of the 1961 World Series, the Yankees leading 1-0 with two outs in the bottom of the ninth, Matty Alou on third, Willie Mays on second. Tino Martinez doing that little jump after he hit a grand slam off Mark Langston to break a 5-5 tie in the bottom of the seventh in Game One of the 1998 World Series. Yet what remains most vivid are those two losses. Baseball is about suffering, even for Yankees fans.

I am a Yankees fan because my father was a Yankees fan. For me, and for so many, the relationship to the team, and hence that sense of identity, is inextricable from the relationship to one's father. He was born in Brooklyn, playing sandlot baseball in Canarsie, but he was always a fan of the Yankees, going to the Bronx to watch Ruth,

Gehrig, and DiMaggio. He was a fighter pilot and ace in World War Two, flying P-40s and P-51s in China. He stayed in the newly formed Air Force after the war, serving as a test pilot for the first jets at Eglin Field in Florida, sometimes flying an F-86 Sabre Jet to St. Petersburg to watch the Yankees in spring training. The Air Force sent him to Cal Tech to study aeronautical engineering when I was four years old. On October 8, 1956, he ran into class to tell everyone that Don Larsen had just pitched a perfect game, only to receive perplexed stares from his professor and classmates. He explained that they preferred the Fourier series to the World Series.

My father was a Yankees fan to his dying day. In February 2008 he suffered the heart attack that would eventually kill him. When I got the news, I immediately flew to Washington and took a taxi directly to the hospital. When I walked into the ICU, he took off his oxygen mask and said, "Did the Yankees invite Doug Mientkiewicz [a utility first baseman, lifetime BA .271] to spring training?"

My father taught me how to throw a baseball. Like so many fathers and sons over the decades, we would play catch every summer night before my mother called us in for dinner. I played in Little League when I was growing up, the low point coming when I was in the third grade. The coach put me in to pitch and I could not throw a strike, walking in run after run. The umpire was my father. I remember crying in the car as we drove back home, asking him why he wouldn't give me the outside corner.

I eventually got over it. When I went to college, he gave me his glove, a 1960 Rawlings six-finger glove, with a "deep-well pocket," the Bob Turley model. Turley (lifetime ERA 3.64) pitched for the Yankees. We played catch on the beach in Florida on his eightieth birthday, with my father using that glove.

Yankee Stadium opened in 1923, the year my father was born. It closed in 2008, the year he died. Back when there was a place called DC Stadium and a team called the Senators, he and I would be there when the Yankees came to town; we never missed a twi-night doubleheader. We always sat in the upper deck along the first-base line, both for its vantage point of the field of play and so we had a good view of the visitors' dugout, where we could see Mickey Mantle and Roger Maris and Elston Howard (I could provide the entire 1963 lineup, but will not).

He and I watched hundreds of games together on television, and as I have watched the Yankees since he died, I can hear his voice; I know exactly what he would say about each pitch and each play. When I was a kid, he sometimes used terms that people don't use anymore, for good reason, terms like "Chinese home run" to describe a ball that barely clears the fence, a term he learned from listening to the announcers at the Polo Grounds. There were many such home runs when Yankee Stadium was only 295 feet down the right field line, but somehow they were hit only by opposing players like Rocky Colavito. When Mickey hit one, my father would say, "He didn't get it all, but it still went out."

On June 5, 1963, the Yankees were playing the Orioles at Memorial Stadium. In the bottom of the sixth, Brooks Robinson hit a deep drive to center field. Back then, the center field "wall" was a chain link fence. When Mickey Mantle leapt to try to catch the ball, his cleats caught in the fence. When he fell to the ground, he broke a metatarsal bone and tore ligaments in his left foot. He was supposed to be out for the season.

On August 4, the Orioles were at Yankee Stadium. The Yankees were trailing 10-9 in the bottom of the seventh when Ralph Houk called on Mantle to pinch-hit for pitcher Steve Hamilton. I was eleven years old, listening to the Baltimore broadcast of the game on WBAL on my transistor radio. Chuck Thompson was calling the game. In Mantle's first at bat since the devastating injury, he hit a game-tying home run. The Yankees went on to win the game in the tenth inning. From New York, the Yankees came to Washington for a four-game series with the Senators. My father and I went to the night game, August 7, which the Yankees won 9-1. Al Downing pitched a complete game (so common in that golden age), giving up only three hits. Mantle did not play at all that entire series, which concluded with an afternoon game on August 8.

In those days, teams flew on commercial jets, not private planes. My father, who was still in the Air Force, learned that the Yankees would be departing after the game to fly out to Los Angeles to play the Angels, leaving from Dulles Airport. My mother drove my friend Jimmer Stewart (not a Yankee fan) and me out to Dulles, each with a baseball in our hand. Back then, there was no TSA, no airport security. We stood in front of the gate and watched through the large windows at the front of the airport. A bus pulled up and my Yankees filed out, each dressed in a coat and tie. I immediately recognized each from his baseball card.

I figured that I might be able to get two autographs as they walked by. The question was who. I spotted Yogi Berra, who was playing his last season with the Yankees that year. He was not his usual loveable self that day, scowling as I approached and said, "Mr. Berra, would you sign my ball?" He did. Joe Pepitone passed by, glaring at me for not asking for his autograph—because I had spotted my hero, bringing up the rear. He was on crutches, despite having hit the pinch-hit homer against the Orioles a few days before. He was flanked by two large men. Getting up my nerve, I approached him and asked for his autograph. He stopped, set his crutches aside, and signed the ball.

I had gotten DiMaggio's autograph a few years before when he visited the Air Force Academy (where my father was teaching thermodynamics) and posed with our Little League teams. I have the group photo somewhere, the children in their team T-shirts and caps, kneeling around DiMaggio, who had retired in 1951, in his Yankee pinstripes, Number 5. But I never saw DiMaggio play; I only heard my father talk about his beautiful swing, his fluid gait around the bases, and his legendary grace in the outfield, never seeming to strain, catching long flies and line drives in full stride. I had seen Berra and Mantle play many times, and Mantle was always my hero. Now I had their autographs on my ball.

After the Yankees boarded the plane, we ran outside and got in the car, where my mother was waiting. I excitedly showed her the ball. I asked Jimmer, "Who did you get?" He did not know the team the way I did and had just approached the first player he saw. After he signed the ball, the player said, "Do you know who I am, kid?" When Jimmer confessed that he did not, he said, "You just got the bat boy's autograph." "Let me see that," I said, grabbing the ball. It said, "Jim Bouton."

My father and I continued to go to see the Yankees

play the Senators during the dismal seasons of the late 1960s and after Mickey's retirement in 1968. In 1970, I left for college at the University of Virginia. I confess that I stopped following baseball closely during my undergraduate years. The sports section of the local paper, *The Daily Progress*, did not have good baseball coverage and I had essentially stopped watching television. It was also the time of the Vietnam War, when so many national institutions fell out of fashion with America's youth, including baseball. The Yankees were not very good then and the favorite players of my childhood had either retired or been traded. In 1972, the Washington Senators became the Texas Rangers. My hometown lost its team and my father and I could not easily see the Yankees play anymore.

It was during this time that, like so many of my generation, my interests turned to the East and I began to study Buddhism, studying both Sanskrit and Tibetan as an undergraduate and deciding to pursue more serious study in graduate school, staying on at the University of Virginia to do so. As I look back, I sometimes wonder whether the Yankees' mediocre record during those formative years of my life caused me to ponder the nature of suffering, the first of the Buddha's four noble truths.

Despite my immersion in the mysteries of the mystic East, I was always able to find a television as the Yankees roared back to greatness to win the pennant, losing to the Big Red Machine in 1976 and beating the Dodgers in 1977, with Roy White finally getting a ring. By the fall of 1978, I had completed my master's degree and entered the doctoral program, which required that I spend a year in Asia for my dissertation research. I was ready to go to India on a Fulbright Fellowship, but was able to delay my departure long enough to see Graig Nettles catch Carl Yastrzemski's foul pop to end the one-game playoff, remembered for Mickey Rivers' bat in Bucky Dent's hands and Lou Piniella's decoy.

I left for India the next day and so missed both the ALCS against the Royals and the World Series; I had to go to the American Embassy in New Delhi to read the line scores in the *International Herald Tribune*, learning that the Yankees had defeated the Dodgers in six games, the series remembered especially for Nettles' stellar defense at third. Living in a Tibetan monastery in South India the following spring, I remember reading every word of *The Sporting News* that my father had sent me, poring over the batting averages from the Carolina League as I sat on my rope bed under a single bare lightbulb in my monk's cell.

In 1980, I began my first academic job. The Yankees lost to George Brett and the Royals in the ALCS, three games to none. The next year, they lost the World Series to the Dodgers a few weeks after my daughter was born. As a new father, I didn't follow the Yankees that closely for the next few years, watching only the numbers of Don Mattingly, he of the coiled-cobra swing and the patented three-hops-to-the-wall-opposite-field-line-drive doubles, a player of such grit and such class that I would never refer to him as "Donnie Baseball."

My job was at Middlebury College in Vermont, which was both a blessing and a curse. It was a curse because Vermont was one of the northern provinces of "Red Sox Nation." I generally kept my allegiance to the Yankees to myself. Like most Yankees fans, I loathe the Red Sox. Over the last few years, I have watched most of the ESPN *30 for 30* documentaries, except the one called "Four Days in October," about the 2004 ALCS. I was in Rome during those games, feeling that I could confidently leave the country with the Yankees up 3-0 in the best-of-seven series, learning of their demise from a newspaper in a hotel in Trastevere. I have never watched the last four games, or clips of those games, and will never watch "Four Days in October." If I am ever captured and interrogated, my captors could do nothing more sadistic than to put those non-blink devices in my eyes, like the ones they used on Alex in *A Clockwork Orange*, and make me watch that documentary.

My time in Vermont was a blessing because baseball had come back to me, or I had come back to baseball, and I found among the faculty a number of people who loved the game as much as I did. The sociologist Rudi

Haerle was a member of SABR—the Society of American Baseball Research—and had an extensive baseball card collection. He was a Cubs fan, so we were able to talk. After the 1986 World Series, the Red Sox fans needed to talk, and I was able to provide a shoulder to cry on, albeit with secret schadenfreude.

A group of us began going to games. Fortunately for me, the nearest major league city to Middlebury was not Boston but Montreal, and we would drive across the border to see the Expos. They were a good team in the mid-1980s, with the Big Cat, Andres Galarraga; Tim "Rock" Raines; Tim Wallach; Vance Law; The Hawk, Andre Dawson; and El Presidente, Dennis Martinez.

The eighties were a good time for baseball fantasy, with films like *The Natural* and *Field of Dreams*. The eternity of baseball, where a game can go on forever, has inspired all manner of fantasy, as it does in W. P. Kinsella's *The Iowa Baseball Confederacy* and *Shoeless Joe* (which was made into *Field of Dreams*). Indeed, because the season is so long, books and films about baseball (unless they are biographies) tend to focus on a single season. In both *Bull Durham* and *The Natural*, as well as the great *Bang the Drum Slowly*, the end of the season provides the denouement, happy or sad.

A less well-known single-season film that I remember watching on a VCR during my early years as a professor is *It Happens Every Spring*, from 1949, in which

Vernon Simpson (played by Ray Milland) is a bespecta-
cled chemistry professor, a fan of St. Louis (whether the
Cardinals or Browns is not specified). One day, while he
is mixing chemicals in his lab, a baseball crashes through
the window, smashing the beakers, the ball rolling
around on the bench and soaking up the different chemicals. The professor discovers that this new concoction
makes the ball repel wood. He goes to the St. Louis
team and requests a tryout, giving his name as "Kelly."
The owner and manager reluctantly agree to the tryout,
then sign him to a contract when this scrawny unknown
strikes out their best hitter; the professor has placed a
tube of the magic chemicals inside his glove, and rubs
the ball with his concoction before he pitches.

Kelly soon becomes "King Kelly," leading St. Louis to
the World Series. He runs out of his magic potion in the
seventh game, but St. Louis wins when Kelly barehands
a line shot back through the box. He holds on, catching
the final out while conveniently breaking his hand and
ending his single-season career. He can now return to
the classroom, be hailed by the students, and marry the
daughter of the college president. In many ways, this
film is the ultimate baseball fantasy, especially for academics, who seem to love baseball more than any other
sport. It is the story of a nerd with no talent, joining a
major-league team with no time spent in the minors,

becoming a star, leading his team to the World Series, and then returning to his nerd life.

In 1989, I joined the faculty at the University of Michigan. Safely out of New England, I could root for the Tigers and their Old English D in good faith, except when they played the Yankees. I know academics who switch their allegiance to the nearest big-league team when they are hired at a new college or university. This has always seemed like blasphemy, apostasy, and treason to me. No matter where I have lived in my life, my devotion to the Yankees has remained unchanged.

What has changed is the way I follow the games. It is no longer necessary to wait for the Yankees to appear on *Game of the Week*, broadcast by Dizzy Dean and Pee Wee Reese (though today we long for broadcasters with nicknames like that). It is no longer necessary to drive around at night trying to pick up games on the car radio or to wait for the Yankees to play the Senators or the Orioles so that I can listen to night games on my transistor radio. I can watch every Yankees game on cable with Comcast's "Extra Innings" package, and when I am away from home, I can watch games on my iPad. I am slightly embarrassed to say that for the past few seasons, I have watched all or part of the 162 regular-season games the Yankees played (and of course every inning of the playoffs).

And having watched the game at night, the next

morning I will watch the "Condensed Game" on the MLB Network app on my iPad, read about the game in *The New York Times*, and follow that up with the more detailed coverage in the *New York Post* (always reading Joel Sherman's column), New York's *Daily News*, and the late lamented website River Avenue Blues. Yet baseball is also a game of nostalgia. Sometimes I miss the exercise in imagination that comes from reliving a game through just a box score in the morning paper.

I have been engaged in the study of Buddhism for fifty years, ten years as a student and forty years as a professor, during which time I have taught scores of courses on Buddhism, written books, translated texts, and compiled a huge dictionary. Over the years, in casual conversation people have told me that this or that "sounds kind of Buddhist" or that almost anything sounds "Zen." I have generally remained unconvinced by these statements, finding them often to express a more generic New Age sentiment than anything I recognize from the vast but specific history of Buddhism. Professional scholars of Buddhism know that Zen was never very Zen, and that the Zen practiced in America is unlike the Zen practiced in Japan, where Zen temples are places people go for funerals for their parents and day care for their children.

It also doesn't mean much to me when an occasional sports star declares himself to be a Buddhist. When Tiger

Woods had an uncanny ability to sink long putts, it was attributed by some to the fact that his Thai mother is a Buddhist. There have been some baseball players who were Buddhists, including great players from my youth: Willie Davis (lifetime BA .279), who played center field for the Dodgers in the 1960s; and Orlando Cepeda (lifetime BA .297), the "Baby Bull," the Hall of Fame first baseman for the Giants, Cardinals, and Braves. They were both Nichiren Buddhists, the ones who chant, *namu myoho rengke kyo*—"Homage to the *Lotus Sutra*."

This book is not about things in baseball that seem Buddhist. It is not about baseball players who are Buddhist, as interesting as such a book might be. This book makes a bolder claim: that the Buddha invented baseball, with the text of his teaching, whose title might be roughly rendered as *The Baseball Sutra*, presented here for the first time. One may scoff at this, knowing that it would be impossible for a game that seems first to have appeared in England in the eighteenth century to have been invented by someone who died in India around 400 B.C. But Buddhists believe that the Buddha is omniscient, with full knowledge of the past, present, and future. Buddhists believe that the Buddha teaches what is appropriate for a given time and place. Buddhists believe that the Buddha left teachings behind, buried in the earth, to be discovered at the appropriate moment in cosmic history.

When the old Yankee Stadium was demolished in 2010, workers uncovered what appeared to be an ancient scroll. They took it to the New York Public Library, where it was revealed to be a Sanskrit text, bearing the title *Daṇḍakanduka Sūtra*. The title of the text is a compound made from two Sanskrit words: *daṇḍa*, which means a staff or a cudgel, and *kanduka*, which is the word for a ball used in games. After deciphering the scroll, scholars have concluded that *daṇḍakanduka* is most accurately translated as "baseball." The word *sūtra*, which usually means "aphorism," is the standard term for a discourse of the Buddha. All textual and contextual evidence suggests that this scroll is an accurate record of the teaching of the historical Buddha. In *Buddha Takes the Mound*, this sutra is translated into a modern language for the first time.

Buddhism is my profession and baseball is my passion. Over the years, I have come to believe that the Buddha invented baseball to teach us deep truths—truths about the world, about ourselves, about each other. I believe that Buddhism provides a lens for us to see baseball in a new way, a way that makes us love the game even more, a way that makes us ponder profound questions about winning and losing, about who we are, about finitude and infinitude, about birth and death. This book reveals not simply that Buddhism is integral to baseball, that Buddhism is inherent in baseball, but that baseball *is* Buddhism. We just didn't know it until now.

THE BASEBALL SUTRA,
WITH COMMENTARY

THE PROLOGUE

Thus did I hear. At one time, the Buddha was residing in the pure land called Yankee Stadium in the city of New York in the land of America in the Western Continent. As he stood near the center of the green mandala, a great rumbling was heard. Beneath his flat feet, each marked with the image of a ball, a great mountain rose from the earth, a full fourteen finger breadths in height. Around that mountain, a smaller mandala in the shape of a diamond magically appeared, with a border of sand from the River Ganges, a cushion of the finest Benares silk at three corners. Atop the great mountain there was a slab of alabaster, pure white in color, two cubits long and eight finger breadths wide. Here the Buddha stood.

The mountain was surrounded by a great assembly of immortals, gods, and demigods of the past and the present, each gathered at his position in the ten directions of the pure land. At the first square in the east stood Gehrig, Moose, Pepitone, Mattingly, and Martinez. At the second square in the north stood Richardson,

Randolph, Soriano, and Canó. At the third square in the west stood McDougald, Boyer, Nettles, and Brosius. At the place between the second square and the third square stood Rizzuto, Kubek, and Jeter. At the place called the household in the south crouched Berra, Howard, Munson, and Posada, each adorned with the tools of ignorance, each flashing signs. In the place called the right in the northeast stood Ruth, Maris, Jackson, Sweet Lou, O'Neill, Godzilla, and Judge. In the place called the center in the north stood DiMaggio, Mantle, Murcer, and Bernie. In the place called the left in the northwest stood White, Winfield, and Gardner. Standing at the foot of the mountain, surrounding the Buddha, stood Ford, Reynolds, Gomez, Terry, Stottlemyre, Gator, Catfish, Key, Pettitte, Cone, Boomer, El Duque, Moose, Sabathia, and Mo. To the Buddha's left side in a narrow cave dug out of the earth sat Stengel, Houk, Showalter, and Torre.

Beyond the field sat row upon row of laymen and laywomen, reaching almost to the heavens. In the row nearest to the field sat the laymen named Rickey and Miller. High above in a box sat the preachers Barber, Allen, McCarver, Singleton, Kay, Sterling, and Waldman, the scribes Angell, Verducci, Madden, Olney, Kepner, and Sherman. In another box sat men called Stick and Cash. Seated alone high above was the one of gentle voice and perfect pronunciation of all names in all languages, called the Herder of Sheep.

At that time, without speaking, the Buddha performed a mudra that united the opposites. He did not need a glove; all buddhas have webbed fingers. His right hand made the gesture of the circle change. The index finger of his left hand pointed down, calling for a fastball, then two fingers pointing down for a curveball, then three fingers pointing down for a slider. And then, he emitted a ray of light from between his eyebrows that illuminated all ten directions from the three divisions of east, central, and west of the American and the National, from the highest heavens of the major leagues to the deepest hells of Low A.

All the gods in the pure land and the laypeople in the stands were perplexed by this sight. The bodhisattva called The Baby said to the bodhisattva called The Horse of Iron, "I have long dwelled in this pure land, yet never have I seen the Buddha perform such a miracle. I ask you to explain it to me, you who followed me in the line and who brought me home so many times." The Horse of Iron replied, "It was a long ago, in another pure land called the Old Yankee Stadium where it was only 295 down the right field line. You were there that day but you do not remember, for between innings you had eaten many hot dogs. On that day, the Buddha also emitted a ray of light from between his eyebrows, illuminating all the leagues in the ten directions. Then he preached what is called *The Baseball Sutra*. I believe he will now preach that *Baseball Sutra* again."

Then the bodhisattva known as Seven stood, put on his batting helmet, and addressed the Buddha: "Lord, in the past when you set forth *The Baseball Sutra*, the gods of this pure land named Yankee Stadium lived their whole lives in this abode, unless they were banished to Kansas City. At that time, as the Buddha of our pure land, you taught this precious sutra only to us. Having meditated on your teaching in the clubhouse, during batting practice, in the on-deck circle, during rainouts, and in the dugout, we your devoted disciples went from victory to victory, defeating our enemies in four, five, six, or seven games. Today, because of free agency, our enemies become our friends, our friends become our enemies. Thus, I beseech you to teach *The Baseball Sutra* to all the gods of all the pure lands."

The Buddha smiled upon the Commerce Comet, saying, "Well done, well done, child of good slugging percentage, wearer of the Triple Crown. You speak the truth. In the world of baseball on this day, among the gods, there is no friend or enemy. It is only the multitudes who abide in the bleachers who bear enmity throughout their lifetimes. Therefore, I shall teach *The Baseball Sutra* to all the gods."

The laymen and laywomen seated on the borders of the mandala began to boo, each in their own language, silenced only when The Baby stood to speak. Adjusting his jockstrap, he addressed the Buddha: "Lord, I do not understand. Your pure land is full, its field filled with Yankees, its seats filled with fans. Our abbots sit in the dugout. The only empty space is the dugout of our enemies, who abide there only for three days or four days, or one day to make up a rainout. Yet the gods of the other pure lands are many. There is no space to fit the gods of the Eastern Division of the American League, much less the gods of all the divisions of all the leagues."

The Buddha replied, "Did you come for the dharma or did you come for the dugout? Bambino, you should know that the powers of the Buddha are inconceivable, able to fill the visitors' dugout with all of the gods of the other pure lands, without changing the size of the gods and without changing the size of the dugout." The Buddha again emitted rays of light from the space between his eyes, the color of a blue pinstripe. Yet, as if by a miracle, as those rays approached the other pure lands, they turned into the color of that pure land—blue for the pure land of the Dodgers, red for the pure land of the Cardinals, green for the pure land of the A's, orange for the pure land of the Mets.

As they reached those pure lands, the rays of light were transformed into all manner of gifts for the gods:

gloves, bats, cleats, batting helmets, batting gloves, elbow protectors, catcher's masks, car dealerships, deodorant commercials, and postgame radio shows. Delighted, the gods of the other pure lands boarded their team planes and flew to the city of New York, landing there in the time it takes for a man to bend his arm. After an hour spent in traffic, they arrived at the pure land called Yankee Stadium.

First to enter the stadium were the gods from Boston, led by The Kid, a god who does not tip his cap. He was followed by gods named Yaz, Tiant, Evans, Lynn, Big Papi, and Pedro. From Baltimore came gods named Palmer, Boog, Murray, Cal, and two gods named Robinson. From Seattle came gods named the Big Unit, Junior, Edgar, and Ichiro. From Detroit came Kaline, Freehan, Lolich, Trammell, Whitaker, and Verlander. From San Francisco came Mays, Marichal, McCovey, Cepeda, Clark, and Posey. From Minnesota came Oliva, Killebrew, Kaat, Carew, and Mauer. From Philadelphia came gods named Lefty, Allen, Schmidt, Rollins, and Utley. From Milwaukee came gods named The Hammer, Mathews, Spahn, Yount, and Molitor. From the pure land of Montreal came gods named Vlad, Rock, The Hawk, and Carter. From Toronto came Alomar, Halladay, Delgado, and He of the Constant Helmet. From St. Louis, gods named The Man, Gibson, Boyer, Simmons, Pujols, Molina, and the Wizard of Oz. From Cleveland,

Colavito, Thome, and Omar. From Pittsburgh, Clemente, Stargell, Parker, and McCutchen. From Queens, gods named Seaver, Straw, Doc, Hernandez, and Wright. From one Los Angeles, Koufax, Drysdale, Fernando, Hershiser, Piazza, and Kershaw. From the other Los Angeles, Grich, Joyner, and the fish, Salmon and Trout. From Houston, Bagwell, Biggio, and Richard. From Oakland, Rickey, Rudi, and Blue. From one Chicago, Banks, Santo, Buckner, Sandberg, Jenkins, and Wood. From the other Chicago, gods named Minnie, Little Louie, Baines, and the Big Hurt. From Atlanta, gods named Murphy, Chipper, Smoltz, Glavine, Mad Dog, and Crime Dog. From Cincinnati, Pinson, Flood, Bench, and Morgan. From Texas, Von Ryan's Express and Pudge. From Kansas City, Brett, McRae, Saberhagen, and Bo. From San Diego, a god named Tony. From the old Washingtons, the Big Train, Hondo, Brinkman, and Osteen. From Tampa came Longoria, Price, and Crawford. From Miami came Sheffield, Cabrera, and Leiter. From Arizona, came Schilling, Grace, and Finley. From Colorado came Walker, Helton, and Bichette. And from an ancient league came gods named Satchel, Josh, Buck, and Cool Papa. Finally, summoned by the Buddha from the realm of the hungry ghosts, came a god with no shoes.

When all the gods had found their places in the dugout, the Buddha declared: "Now, I will set forth

The Baseball Sutra for the benefit of the many, for the happiness of the many, out of compassion for the world, for the welfare, the benefit, and the happiness of players and fans." Yet before he could begin, five hundred gods stood up and made their way across the field toward the bullpen exit. Among them were gods named Rocket, Barry, Big Mac, Sammy, A-Rod, Manny, Rafael, Miguel, Vaughn, Brown, Braun, and the King of Hits. Others rose to stop them, but the Buddha said, "Let them go. It will be many eons before they enter nirvana." Thus spoke the Buddha.

THE QUESTION

Then, by the power of the Buddha, the yogi named Berra stood, lifted his mask, and addressed the Buddha. "Lord, as you stood atop the mountain forty cubits from where I squat, you showed first one finger, then two fingers, then three. He who catches the ball must make these signs from behind the white platter. Yet the Blessed One made them toeing the slab atop the mountain. I am confused. Please explain the meaning of these three signs."

The Buddha replied, "Well said, well said, notorious bad-ball hitter, three-time MVP. What you say is true. Now, listen to my words: When I made three signs from atop the mountain, their meaning was not fastball, curveball, and slider. They had a hidden meaning, a meaning that I reveal to you this day. Just as there are three strikes, so there are three signs that mark everything in the lives of players and fans. What are those three? They are impermanence, suffering, and no self. I teach these three signs so that all beings may be liberated from sorrow and find the peace of nirvana.

"Yet these three signs are difficult to understand for those of low OPS. And so I have created this game called baseball, played in the diamond realm, so that gods and humans might understand and find peace. It is the game of odd numbers: three outs, three strikes, nine innings, twenty-seven outs. It is the best of games, superior to the games of the unenlightened, for it teaches that the cycle of birth and death is endless, extending to infinity. Like the cycle of birth itself, the game can last forever. The games of the unenlightened have quarters and halves, shot clocks and two-minute warnings. In baseball, there can be extra innings extending over innumerable eons. The highest possible ERA for the caster of ball is infinity. And why? If he is lifted in his first start with even one run scored without an out being recorded, the ERA is infinity. The number of strikeouts possible in a single inning is infinity. And why? If the batter reaches base on a wild pitch or passed ball on the third strike, the maximum number of strikeouts is infinity. The number of pitches a batter can foul off with two outs and two strikes in the bottom of the ninth is infinity. The number of innings that the teams can play is infinity.

"Yet just as a plantain tree grows, abides, decays, and dies, so does each game have its phases of early innings, middle innings, late innings, and the final out. Dying and reborn, the teams play again the next day (unless it rains), 162 times, as many as 183 if there is a tie-breaker and they go to what is renowned as the seventh game. And then there's always next year." Thus spoke the Buddha.

Commentary

The Buddha is said to have always adapted his teachings to the interests, needs, and capacities of his disciples. Like a doctor, he did not prescribe the same medicine for all maladies, but instead taught each person what was most appropriate for them. He responded to the needs of others. For this reason, his discourses, called sutras (a Sanskrit word originally meaning "aphorism"), after setting the scene (as in the previous chapter), often begin when a member of the audience, usually a monk, rises from his seat, bows to the Buddha, and, with his palms joined in a gesture of reverence, asks the Buddha a question. The sutra, regardless of its length, is the Buddha's answer to this question and other questions that might be asked by other members of the audience.

Here in *The Baseball Sutra*, the audience is the assembled baseball stars from ages past and present and the fans filling the seats in Yankee Stadium. The question is asked by Yogi Berra, Number 8, the legendary Yankee catcher during the team's glory years of the 1950s and '60s. In Buddhism, ignorance is said to be at the root of all suffering. So it is appropriate that the question be asked by someone who is adorned with "the tools of ignorance," the term used to describe the catcher's equipment: the chest protector, the mask, the shin guards, the cup. In Buddhist art, the Buddha is depicted with his hands in different positions, called *mudrās*, each of which has a symbolic meaning. One is a gesture with his right hand called "turning the wheel of the dharma"—that is, teaching. Another is called "bestowing fearlessness."

Here, the Buddha has not displayed any of the usual gestures that we know from Buddhist art, but instead has made gestures that seem to call for a fastball, a curve, and a slider. Yogi Berra, having caught 1,694 games and called thousands of pitches as a Yankee, understands the signs well. But the signs are to be made by the catcher, not by someone standing on the pitcher's mound. Hence, he is understandably puzzled and asks the Buddha what these signs mean.

The Buddha famously taught that all things carry what are called "the three marks" (akin to the three strikes): impermanence, suffering, and no self; that everything we encounter, as well as our bodies and minds, is constantly changing and therefore is impermanent; that because everything can cause us pain, everything is a potential source of suffering; and that we wrongly believe that we possess some kind of essence, some kind of self, when in fact there is no self.

The Buddha will devote the next three chapters of *The Baseball Sutra* to impermanence, suffering, and no self, setting forth his teachings and finding their most perfect expression in baseball. The ignorant believe that things are permanent, that they are sources of happiness, and that they have a self. This misunderstanding, this ignorance, is, according to Buddhism, what keeps people locked in a cycle of suffering and prevents them from finding freedom. The Buddha says that in order to convey his teachings, to teach these truths, truths said to be difficult to understand by those of this benighted world, he has invented the game of baseball. It is typical for the Buddha to praise what he is about to teach as a means of inspiring his audience to pay close attention. Thus, before he begins *The Baseball Sutra*, he explains what is unique about baseball, why it is the most profound game, why baseball is the best of all games.

He begins with the question of time. One of the unusual features of the Buddha's teaching is that, unlike so many other philosophies, he does not talk about origins and end times, about how the universe began and how it will end. When time is mentioned in Buddhist scriptures, it is almost always in minute or vast measures, in instants or eons, very rarely in years. It is a basic tenet of Buddhism that existence, called *saṃsāra* (literally, "wandering"), has no beginning, that all of the beings in the universe—gods in their heavens; humans on the earth; animals and insects of the land, sea, and sky; ghosts; and the denizens of subterranean hells—have all been reborn an infinite number of times in the past and that they will continue to be reborn infinitely in the future until they find the path to escape from the cycle, the path known only by the Buddha.

To help us understand the idea of this endless cycle of suffering, he has invented the game of baseball, where a single game can, at least hypothetically, go on forever. There is no end to extra innings if no team is ahead when the third out is recorded at the bottom of the inning. Like samsara, the game goes on and on, unless there's a rainout.

Infinity appears elsewhere in baseball, in ways that lead only to despair. Consider the poor pitcher in the first start of the season who gives up a run and is taken out before the first out is recorded. His earned run average is infinity. Strikeouts are the pitcher's *pièce de résistance*, with strikeouts per game, strikeouts per season, and strikeouts in a career each a major measure of a pitcher's greatness. Baseball fans await one of the rarest of events, the "immaculate inning," in which a pitcher throws only nine pitches, all strikes (accomplished by Sandy Koufax three times). Idolized strikeout pitchers like Walter

Johnson, Nolan Ryan, Randy Johnson, Steve Carlton, and Bob Gibson are among the immortals seated at the Buddha's feet when he sets forth *The Baseball Sutra*.

And yet, the immaculate inning can go on forever, turning fame into infamy. This would happen when, with no one on first or with two outs, the third strike to each batter was a swinging strike at a wild pitch or passed ball, or even a called strike that eluded the catcher. Batter after batter would strike out, run to first before the catcher could throw him out, and then come around to score, the pitcher breaking the strikeout record for a nine-inning game (twenty, jointly held by Roger Clemens, Kerry Wood, and Max Scherzer) before the end of the first inning. If this was his first outing and he was removed (as he likely would be) before the first out was recorded and each third strike came on a wild pitch, his ERA would be infinity, despite never giving up a walk or a hit. The Buddha provides this as one of the many examples of infinity in baseball. Later, he will use the same situation as an example of the suffering of change, how those things that are ordinarily a cause of pleasure (for instance, the strikeout for a pitcher) become a source of pain.

Having given several examples of infinity—of how, unlike most other sports, baseball is not bound by time—the Buddha turns to the topic of finitude: how games play out in time and then are played again. He gives an example of impermanence, which he will return to in more depth in the next chapter of the sutra. That example is a plantain tree—a banana tree—a favorite example in Buddhist literature because it is a tree that has no wood. The woodsman seeking firewood fells the plantain tree with his axe, only to find that it has no heartwood, but is just layer after layer of soft stem, with nothing solid, no essence. This makes it a perfect metaphor for the idea of no self, which the Buddha will set forth in the fifth chapter of *The Baseball Sutra*.

Here, however, the plantain tree is simply the example of something that grows, remains for a while, begins to decay, and dies, true for a human being as much as for a tree. And so it is in baseball, where a game begins with great anticipation for players and fans alike; moves into the middle innings, where, unless it is a blowout, the outcome remains in doubt; and then moves to the ninth, where, whether a squeaker or a laugher, one team is defeated, one pitcher takes the loss, one reliever may blow the save. And this goes on day after day after day for six months, not counting the early reporting of pitchers and catchers, not counting spring training itself, not counting all the rounds of the playoffs. This game that the Buddha invented provides endless opportunities to contemplate loss.

Yet this game which is so fraught with suffering has

become the "national pastime" of a great nation and, like the teachings of the Buddha, has spread around the world. Both the popularity of baseball and the popularity of Buddhism seem somehow improbable.

Buddhism began as a small movement of wandering monks in northeast India 2,500 years ago, yet today it is counted a "world religion," with millions of adherents and millions more admirers around the globe. Indeed, when the term "world religion" was coined (in German) in the nineteenth century, only two religions were counted: Christianity and Buddhism. Other religions began in similar ways, but what is particularly interesting about Buddhism is that it was just one of dozens of ascetic movements in ancient India, yet it was the only one to survive and spread far beyond India.

And it did so against remarkable odds, crossing mountains, deserts, oceans, and language barriers. Buddhism has a large technical vocabulary, in the difficult language of classical India, Sanskrit; and its many texts had to be translated into many languages, first across Asia and today around the world. This was a challenging task for a number of reasons. In Buddhism, ordinary terms are given technical meanings. One thinks immediately of the four noble truths: suffering, origin, cessation, and path. But Buddhism also has its own concocted terms, unique to it, terms that are difficult to translate into English (or any other language), terms like "dependent origination," "non-associated compositional factor," and "immediately preceding condition."

Long ago, George Carlin brilliantly described the differences between baseball and football, calling baseball "a nineteenth-century pastoral game" and football "a twentieth-century technological struggle." The language of baseball is strikingly simple, composed primarily of one-and two-syllable terms, almost all with a domestic connotation—perhaps not surprising, when the goal of the game is to reach home safely. These are terms that most Americans, at least of the last century, would understand and use in daily life. Yet in baseball, these terms have an additional meaning, unrelated to their original denotation.

In many cases, these terms are not metaphors. They are instead a private language for a separate universe, incomprehensible to all but the initiated. One thinks, for example, of "room service," "can of corn," "kitchen," "cup of coffee," "rope," "airmail," "bleeder," "chin music," "foot in the bucket," "gas," "hot corner," "hung out to dry," "late life," "cookie," "pickle," "rabbit ears," "rocking chair," "skip rope," "snow cone," "visitation rights," and "good morning, good afternoon, and good night." The list could go on and on. Describing a line drive, Ken Singleton has been heard to say, "You could hang a week's worth of laundry on that if you didn't have a dryer." It is a game in which "stuff" is a technical term.

Baseball generally lacks the kind of phrases composed of multisyllabic Latinate abstract nouns that make up the vocabulary of football: "illegal substitution," "unnecessary roughness," "unbalanced line," "encroachment," "neutral zone infraction," "intentional grounding." The relatively recent introduction of "defensive indifference" into the baseball lexicon was a clear violation of the spirit of the game.

When Buddhism, with its own specialized language, spread from India to China and beyond, sometimes the Indian terms were translated, often very roughly, into Chinese. In other cases, there were no words in Chinese that were equivalents and so new words were made up that tried to approximate the sound of the Sanskrit. For example, in Chinese, "nirvana" is *niepan*; in Japanese, the word for "Buddha" is *butsu*. In Mongolian, the family name of the Buddha, "Shakyamuni," is *sagamoni*.

Baseball has something of a parallel story—a game of ancient, and rather murky, British origins becoming the quintessential American game, "America's pastime," with so many elements that seem distinctly American, beginning with its arcane vocabulary. This language would seem incomprehensible to someone who did not grow up in the United States—and the United States of a particular time, long past, watching countless games with my father, who would initiate me into the secret language, explaining what the announcer meant when he said there were "ducks on the pond."

And yet baseball has spread around the world: to Latin America, to Japan, and to Korea.

In Spanish, the American words were usually translated: an outfielder is a *jardinero*, a gardener; a strike is a *bola buena*, a good ball; a strikeout is a *ponche*, a punch. When the late lamented Expos played in Montreal, there needed to be a baseball lexicon in French, one that often seemed more formal and less evocative than that of Spanish; the batter's box was *la boîte du frappeur* but "pinch hitter" was the wonderful *le frappeur d'urgence*.

But baseball did not travel just to the other nations of the Northern and Southern Hemispheres, but across the vast ocean, to Korea, Taiwan, and Japan. As in the case of Buddhism, it was necessary to attempt to reproduce the sound of many terms when there was no term that was a rough equivalent. In Japanese, bunt is *banto*, changeup is *chenji appu*, full count is *furu kaunto*, line drive is *raina*, and passed ball is *pasu boru*.

Japan received Buddhism from Korea, but Korea received baseball from Japan. As in Japanese baseball, the Koreans mix translation (using the same Japanese terms but with Korean pronunciation) with phonetic rendering of the English. Thus, in Korean, slider is *sŭllaidŏ*, bunt is *pŏnt´u*, and balk is *pok´ŭ*. In Chinese, baseball terms tend to be translated; the game itself is called *bang qiu*, literally "stickball," a translation likely coined without knowledge of the legendary game of New York neighborhoods.

Buddhism would eventually spread beyond India, north to China, Korea, Japan, Tibet, and Mongolia, south to Sri Lanka and all the countries of Southeast Asia. Each of these regions would produce its own Buddhist saints, and some of those saints would make the long journey to India, the Buddhist holy land, to study the dharma.

Baseball spread to Latin America, producing its own local stars. Those who have made the pilgrimage to the holy land of the major leagues are too many to name, but some must be mentioned, beginning with the great Minnie Miñoso. Marichal, Clemente, Cepeda, Aparicio, Perez, Pedro, Edgar Martinez, and Mo are all in the Hall of Fame. Recent Yankee history is filled with great Latin players: Bernie, Mo, El Duque, Posada, Soriano, Canó. And there is Hector Lopez, the great outfielder of my Yankees youth, whose surname I share.

Japanese players came to the majors more recently; memorable Yankees include, of course, Matsui, MVP of the 2009 World Series; Kuroda; Tanaka; and briefly, the great Ichiro. Korean players are fewer, led by Chan Ho Park, who joined the Dodgers in 1994, and more recently Shin-Soo Choo and Hyun-Jin Ryu. Yankee fans remember Diamondbacks reliever Byung-Hyun Kim. And Yankee fans have a special place in their heart for Chien-Ming Wang of Taiwan, whose career essentially ended when he was rounding third.

And so Buddhism and baseball are examples of the local becoming the global, the national becoming international, the particular becoming universal, the finite becoming infinite. This can happen only because of a certain appeal—or perhaps simply because both baseball and Buddhism are true. Indeed, as the Buddha declares from the mound of Yankee Stadium, he invented baseball to teach the truths of Buddhism and to lead the suffering to salvation. Those truths must be presented in a setting.

In Buddhism, that setting is the world of rebirth, a world that has no beginning and no end, a world created by the past deeds of its denizens. It is on such a stage, where things seem always beyond our control, that the Buddha both revealed the true nature of the world and proclaimed the path to escape it. It is on this stage that the drama of enlightenment is played.

The Buddha invented baseball as a simpler stage to teach his truths, one made of earth and grass, with some lime for the lines, three bags and a plate at the four corners, a little mound, a fence ringing the field. With a bat and a ball, one has everything that one needs to learn the most profound truths.

The required distances are only two: ninety feet and sixty feet six inches, each easily paced off. These distances could not be the design of a mere mortal; only an enlightened being could know that these apparently arbitrary distances would define the perfect measures for teaching the truth of suffering. Only a Buddha could know that not even the fastest runner of the nineteenth, twentieth, or twenty-first century, wearing the best cleats, could beat out a well-hit ground ball to first, second, third, or short. The runner is always out. The distance between the mound and the plate (even when the mound was lowered from fifteen inches to ten inches after Bob Gibson had an ERA of 1.12 in 1968) has ensured over the centuries that hitting a major league pitch is the most difficult feat in all of sport. Only a Buddha would design a game in which those who fail to get a hit 70 percent of the time year after year over a long career end up in the Hall of Fame. It is a game ideal for conveying the truths of Buddhism. Indeed, it was invented to do so.

The most famous truths of Buddhism are the four noble truths, which are said to be the first thing that the Buddha taught when he achieved enlightenment after staying up all night meditating under a tree. At dawn, on his thirty-fifth birthday, he was "awakened"; in Sanskrit, *buddha* means "awakened one." After seven weeks spent savoring his enlightenment, he set out to find his first disciples: five old friends who had rejected him when he abandoned their practice of fasting. He found them living in a park—a game preserve called a "deer park" near the holy city of Benares. There he taught the four noble truths.

The Buddha expounds on each of these in *The Baseball Sutra*. To describe them briefly here, the first truth is that all is suffering. As the Buddha will explain, this does not mean that we are racked by pain during every moment of our existence. He means, instead, that there are sorrows that strike all humans. He lists eight: birth, aging, sickness, death, losing friends, making enemies, not finding what you are looking for, and finding what you are not looking for. The second truth is that this suffering has a cause. In his first sermon, he identifies this cause as "craving" or "thirst," wanting things that we think will bring us contentment, when in fact they always bring disappointment. In other teachings, and here in *The Baseball Sutra*, he identifies the cause as ignorance. By ignorance, he does not mean just not knowing something; he means not understanding who we really are.

The third truth is called "cessation." This means that it is possible to make suffering stop, not just temporarily but forever; it is possible to make suffering impossible. The word that he uses to name this state of cessation is the most famous word in Buddhism: nirvana. Exactly what and where nirvana is has puzzled Buddhist philosophers for centuries. In *The Baseball Sutra*, the Buddha reveals its true location: Cooperstown, New York. Enshrined there are the "contact relics," those things that have touched the body of the saint: the bat, the ball, the glove, the cap, the cleats—just as the Buddha's robe and begging bowl are enshrined in pagodas.

The fourth of the four noble truths is the simple word "path," so rich in meanings, both real and metaphoric. Sadly for us, the path to nirvana is not Interstate 87 but something more elusive, a mystical state that the Buddha will reveal at the end of *The Baseball Sutra* to the faithful gathered around him on the pitcher's mound at Yankee Stadium.

IMPERMANENCE

Then John "Mayor" Lindsey, wearing the uniform of the New Jersey Jackals, rose and addressed the Blessed One. "Lord, I was drafted in the thirteenth round by the Rockies and played A Ball for seven years for the Portland Rockies, the Asheville Tourists, and the Salem Red Sox. Then I was signed by the Mariners and played A Ball for the San Bernardino Stampede before ascending to Double-A, where I played for the San Antonio Missions. Then I descended to the Single-A Jupiter Hammerheads and then to the independent league New Jersey Jackals. Then I signed with the Dodgers and played for the Triple-A Las Vegas 51s and then for their Double-A affiliate, the Jacksonville Suns. Lord, you may know them as the Jacksonville Jumbo Shrimp. Then I signed with the Marlins and played for their Double-A New Orleans Zephyrs. Lord, you may know them as the New Orleans Baby Cakes. Then I signed with the Dodgers again and played for the Triple-A Albuquerque Isotopes of the Pacific Coast League. Lord, after sixteen years in the minors, I was called up by the Dodgers. I wore Dodger Blue for eleven games. I had one hit in twelve at bats before I was hit by a pitch and broke my hand. Later, I was signed by the Tigers and played for the Toledo Mud Hens. And then I was released.

"Blessed One, counting the Mexican League and winter ball, I played 2,277 games in the minors for twenty-five teams over twenty-one years. I drove for endless miles in old buses with bad air-conditioning. I ate countless bad meals of fried food with plastic forks. I loaded countless suitcases on and off buses. I slept in countless bad hotels with stained carpets, coin-operated Magic Fingers beds, and no Wi-Fi. I sat for countless hours on hard benches in concrete dugouts. I took countless showers in cinder-block clubhouses. I played on countless bad fields and played countless bad hops before tiny crowds. And yet my lifetime average in the majors was only .083.

"O Teacher of Players and Fans, taking off my first baseman's mitt, I ask: Why did you make a game so filled with change?"

"O son of the A leagues, I made this game to teach the truth of impermanence, that all things are subject to change, that all things will one day fall apart. I teach that the hot streak leads to the slump, that .300 leads to the Mendoza Line, that the hundred-mile-per-hour heater leads to Tommy John surgery, that the perfect game through six leads to the loss after nine, that the big league contract leads to being designated for assignment.

"I teach the wandering between worlds, where the players in the heavens called the majors are blown by the winds of their statistics to the hells of the minors. I teach that the denizens of Triple A toil in game after game, meeting a god only when that god descends for a rehab assignment and pays for the spread. I teach that even for those who ascend, the time is short, able to wear the garments of the gods only in spring training before being returned to hell, the domain of demeaning team logos.

"I made this game not to make players suffer but to make players see that to be attached to luxury suites, private jets, and Gatorade commercials is only a source of suffering. I made this game to teach players to play without attachment." Thus spoke the Buddha.

Commentary

All religions and much conventional wisdom from cultures around the world and across history speak of the transience of life, that nothing lasts forever, that things fall apart. Heaven and hell, the final destination after death in so many religions, stand in contrast to our inconstant world. In heaven and hell things go on forever, both for the blessed and for the damned. The notion that life is fraught with unexpected and unpredictable change is therefore not unique to Buddhism.

Yet Buddhism is particularly famous for its doctrine of impermanence, and for its detailed exposition of how and why things change and what our response to this fact should be. One of the Buddha's famous aphorisms is "The end of fortune is decline. The end of rising is falling. The end of meeting is parting. The end of birth is death." He is saying that despite whatever success we have in acquiring the things of this world, we will eventually lose them—to our creditors, to the taxman, or to our heirs—no matter how hard we try to hold on to them. That no matter how high we ascend in our fame, our fortune, or our power, we will inevitably fall, often in disgrace. That all of the relationships that we form in life—with our lovers, with our children, with our best friends forever—will inevitably end, often long before our inevitable parting at death. And death is the final change, one that no one can escape, not even the Buddha himself.

In most religions, these changes end at death, as we depart for our final abode in heaven or hell. However, in Buddhism, we are subject to impermanence even there. In Buddhism, heaven and hell are part of samsara, the cycle of birth, death, and rebirth. In Buddhism, the cycle of birth has no beginning; all of us have been reborn countless times in the past. There are six, and only six, possible forms of rebirth: as a god, as a demigod, as a human, as an animal (which includes insects), as a ghost, or as a denizen of hell.

In popular representations, reincarnation is often presented as a chance to come back and do the things you didn't have a chance to do in this life, to be a concert pianist or a rock star. It is often presented as a second chance to get things right. It is this view of reincarnation that has led many people to think that *Groundhog Day* is a Buddhist movie. But in Buddhism, you don't come back as the same person in the next lifetime, and you rarely come back as a human at all. And when you do, it usually doesn't end well. As much as I would like to come back as the center fielder for the Yankees, I could come back as a middle reliever in Double-A who never comes back from Tommy John surgery.

Because in Buddhism rebirth has no beginning, everyone has been everything. There is no place in the universe that we have not lived, there is no species that we have not been. But each of these births ends in death—even birth in heaven or in hell—and we become something else, in a process that seems entirely beyond our control; an insect becomes a god, a god becomes a ghost. The good go to heaven and the bad go to hell, but they do not remain there for eternity. They eventually die there and are reborn someplace else. Eternity is an endless wandering between worlds, to hell and back and then back to hell. Were this not bad enough, we cannot learn from our mistakes, because we cannot remember our previous lives.

It is like baseball, where each season is a lifetime, with players and fans waiting for it to end, wanting it to end, followed by the amnesia of a new rebirth, starting all over again in spring training. Still, some do remember their past lives. In Buddhism, it is said that the denizens of hell remember the misdeed that condemned them to be reborn there, just as the player who has been sent down remembers what sent him there: blowing the save, walking in the winning run, striking out to end the game, failing to run out a grounder.

In Buddhism, each of the six realms of rebirth has its own form of suffering, even for the gods. The denizens of hell suffer the tortures familiar from other religions, in fire and brimstone, but also in frozen wastelands of snow and ice. Ghosts suffer from hunger and thirst. Animals suffer from always being in search of food while always avoiding becoming food. The sufferings of humans are well known to us. Demigods suffer from being jealous of the gods. And gods suffer the premonition of their own demise, an inevitable fall from grace. Other religions speak of similar sufferings, but in Buddhism there is the constant reminder that they can occur at any moment. And this is because of impermanence.

Buddhist texts speak of two kinds of impermanence: coarse and subtle. Coarse impermanence is the change that we observe every day: changes in the weather, in the seasons, in our body, in our moods. We break a teacup, we catch a cold, we get better, we win a prize, we lose a love. These examples of coarse impermanence occur often enough that we should not place confidence in the constancy of anything. And yet we do.

Only the enlightened can see something more profound, called subtle impermanence: the fact that things are constantly in a state of flux, that for those who can see, nothing lasts longer than an instant, whether it is a particle of matter or a moment of thought. A famous Buddhist text compares the constant disintegration of everything in our world to raindrops exploding on a stone courtyard in a downpour. One Buddhist school says that everything, whether mind or matter, passes through three moments, first arising, then abiding for a moment, and then disintegrating in the next moment. Another school offers a more radical view, that arising, abiding, and disintegrating occur constantly, that those terms simply name three perspectives on a single moment.

We, the unenlightened, are not able to see this subtle impermanence, deceived by the illusion of continuity, by the belief that because something looks solid it therefore is solid, that because something seems constant it therefore is constant, something to rely on, something to hold on to. We cannot see that the only thing constant about it is that it is constantly disintegrating. This failure to understand impermanence is a form of ignorance in Buddhism, a religion where ignorance leads to suffering. This is easy enough to understand. When we place our confidence in something and it suddenly falls apart, we are surprised, we feel disappointed, we feel betrayed. We suffer.

But our failure to understand impermanence has far deeper implications in Buddhism. Because we think that things last longer than an instant, we love them. Because we think that things last longer than an instant, we hate them. That desire and that hatred lead us to do things we should not, physical acts like stealing, verbal acts like lying, mental acts like wishing someone harm. These deeds—the Buddhist word for "deed" is *karma*—have effects in the future. Indeed, in Buddhism everything that happens to us—every moment of physical pleasure and physical pain, every moment of mental pleasure and mental pain—is the result of our past deeds.

Buddhists talk about this in the language of seeds and fruit, that the deeds we do in the past are seeds that we plant, seeds that bear the fruit of our experience in the future. Those deeds done in the past could have been done yesterday or millions of lifetimes ago and yet bear their fruit, produce our experience, today. We carry those seeds with us from lifetime to lifetime, with those lifetimes—in heaven or in hell, as a human or an animal— themselves the result of past deeds, as is every moment of pleasure or pain we feel in each of those lifetimes.

We know from our own experience that our joys and sorrows, our physical sensations change constantly. What we don't know is that those changes are the direct result of our past actions, seeds that can bear their fruit at any moment in a process that is completely beyond our control. This is the truth of impermanence, the first of what the Buddha called "the three marks." The other two are suffering and no self. They are called marks because all things bear their imprint. We could also call them "the three strikes." The Buddha invented the game called baseball to teach us about impermanence. As he said, "The end of fortune is decline. The end of rising is falling. The end of meeting is parting. The end of birth is death."

The end of fortune is decline. The term translated as "fortune" here can mean wealth, but it can also mean fortune in a more metaphorical sense, that of being endowed with all manner of skills and powers. In baseball, one thinks immediately of the five-tool player, the position player with exceptional abilities to field, throw, run, hit, and hit with power. Even for the player of great natural ability, these skills are honed over thousands of hours of practice and in hundreds of games, beginning with playing catch to sandlot ball, to Little League, to high school baseball, and then to either college or the minors. And then, with much good fortune, to the majors, where the five-tool player is rewarded with riches, reaching his prime in his middle to late twenties, perhaps peaking around age twenty-nine, and remaining in his prime for a few more years.

But the end of fortune is decline, and in the player's thirties, the tools start to rust, beginning with speed, as the player "loses a step." Bat speed will also decline, with the player no longer able to "catch up to the fastball." Fielders begin to lose their range. Catchers' knees start to go, so they are moved to first or to DH. Pitchers lose a few miles per hour off their fastball, having to learn to be "pitchers" rather than "throwers," mastering and inventing all manner of novelty pitches. (One thinks of David Cone's "Laredo slider.") Eventually, the tools of the major league player will decline so much that he will be traded or released if he wants to spare himself the indignity of being sent down. Unlike in other walks of life, when fortune ends in loss in baseball it is there for all to see, heartbreaking to the fan, as the decline of each skill is meticulously measured, charted, dissected, and discussed. It is a powerful lesson in impermanence.

The end of rising is falling. Every spring, after the Yankees lost their first game of the year, my father would call me and say, "There goes the undefeated season." Given the length of the season and the remarkable range of variables in a given game—whether the pitcher has his "good stuff," whether a batter is "seeing the ball well," whether the manager calls in the right reliever at the right time—falling in the standings is an inevitable part of baseball, with players and fans alike carefully watching how far behind their team is, not in the win column but in the loss column, how many games out of the wild card they are. Almost every team goes on an inexplicable losing streak at some point every year, plummeting in the standings and often falling out of contention. Because bad teams beat good teams so regularly and because the season is so long, teams rise and fall in the standings more dramatically in baseball than in any other sport. It is a powerful lesson in impermanence.

Players rise and fall not just over the course of their career but in the course of a season, with hitters suddenly looking lost at the plate, their batting average plunging below the Mendoza Line, putting them "on the interstate." Relief pitchers have inexplicable bouts of wildness, hitting batters and walking in runs; previously brilliant starters get pounded start after start, having to be lifted in the early innings. Even fielders can be afflicted with the yips—catchers can't throw the ball back to the pitcher; infielders can't throw the ball to first. Cardinal fans recall the struggles of pitcher Rick Ankiel. Yankee fans remember the travails of Gold Glove second baseman Chuck Knoblauch. These descents into the darkness are rarely a case of a decline in skills. They are inexplicable. Or they can be explained by the law of karma. It is a powerful lesson in impermanence.

The end of meeting is parting. Fans my age remember with fondness the time when a substantial portion of the everyday lineup and starting rotation remained with the team for much of their entire career, producing a strong bond of affection and loyalty. Those days ended with the abolition of the reserve clause in 1975; players and fans must always remember the sacrifices of Curt Flood and the efforts of Marvin Miller that led to the end of this form of indentured servitude and greatly enriched players' salaries.

But free agency meant that for both player and fan, meeting and parting began to happen far more often, and that trend has seemed to grow exponentially. As a player makes his way through the various stages of the game, from Little League to the big leagues, he must have thousands of teammates; fifty-four different players were on the Yankees' roster at one time or another in the 2019 season alone. Sometimes a player will be called up for one game, often for a spot start, before being sent down the next day, never to be seen again, at least in the same uniform. How are friendships forged and how are they maintained? How do fans keep track of the team when the twenty-six-man roster is constantly changing? How do they know who the Yankees are without keeping up with all of the minor league affiliates, not just of their home team but of all the teams, whose players may appear in the pinstripes tomorrow?

These are deep questions with profound consequences, consequences that the Buddha will explore in chapter five. But it is clear that there is much meeting in Buddhism, as new players join the major league club and are assigned a number and a locker. And there is much parting, as players leave the team, as they inevitably must. It is a powerful lesson in impermanence.

The end of birth is death. Death has all manner of metaphorical meaning in baseball, some good ("dead pull hitter"), some bad ("dead arm"), and some merely historical ("dead-ball era"). Yet, when the Buddha says that the end of birth is death, he is not speaking metaphorically. Baseball players, even those spoken of in hushed tones as immortals, die. That death can come at any time and it is always something of a shock, even if a player dies as an old man. In some ways, because of the continuity that blinds us to impermanence, we are shocked by any death. But the death of a favorite player, especially a favorite player from one's youth, strikes especially hard. Even if one has not thought about a particular player in the present, that player lives in a past that seems immutable. For Yankee fans of my generation, it was the death of Mickey Mantle that hit the hardest, bringing many grown men to tears. This despite the fact that he was dying of liver failure and the end was surely near. That death immediately sends one to the computer to watch clips of classic games and the cliché-filled sports biography.

The death of the childhood player is also a time to revisit the past. One of my favorite players was Yankees third baseman Clete Boyer, brother of the more famous Ken Boyer of the Cardinals (who died young). Clete was the antithesis of the clean-cut Yankees of the 1960s, often needing a shave, getting into bar fights during spring training. I always thought he was a better fielder than Brooks Robinson, although he never won a Gold Glove while he was with the Yankees. (He finally won one when he moved to the National League, with the Atlanta Braves in 1969.) By the time he died, advanced metrics had been introduced into baseball, and they showed, sadly, that Brooks was slightly better. Still, what remains is the memory of him coming to the plate in the early innings, his uniform dirty from the diving stops he had made at third, throwing from his knees to beat the runner. And yet our heroes die. It is a powerful lesson in impermanence.

However, the Buddha speaks of very few of these things in this chapter of *The Baseball Sutra*. In the other chapters in which he is asked a question by a player, in each case it is a Hall of Famer (or should-be Hall of Famer). But in this chapter on impermanence, his interlocutor is a player who, but for a brief moment, spent his entire career in the minor leagues. And, indeed, it is the complicated cosmos of baseball, with places with names like Low A and winter ball, that best mirrors the

Buddhist universe of samsara, with its gods, its demi-gods, its ghosts, and its denizens of hell. In baseball, the gods in heaven (first place) survey the world below from atop the standings, defeating the demigods (the wild card team) in the playoffs. There are players who are ghosts of their former selves, doomed to be traded before the July 31 deadline as a backup catcher or to join a bullpen as a middle reliever, only to be released when the season ends. And there are the denizens of the hells in various levels of the minor leagues, doomed, as John Lindsey relates in chilling detail, to load one's own luggage into smelly buses, to eat fried food, and to dwell in cheap hotels.

That the end of fortune is decline; that the end of rising is falling; that the end of meeting is parting; that the end of birth is death is nowhere truer than in the minor leagues in this sport called baseball. In many other sports, there is an evolutionary ascent through its various levels, with only rare cases of regression. But in baseball, many players, even very good players, go back and forth between the majors and the minors, even in a single season, living a lifetime of uncertainty, with batters going into slumps and pitchers losing the bite on their cutter. This is a powerful lesson in impermanence.

4

SUFFERING

In the broadcast booth, Kitty took off his headset, rose from his seat next to Bob Costas, and addressed the Buddha. "Lord, in my twenty-five years in the majors, I toed the slab many times. I started 625 games, I won 283 games, I pitched 180 complete games. In those games, I saw so much suffering. I saw pitchers get hammered, throw wild pitches, not have their good stuff, hang curveballs, leave sinkers up in the zone, miss the corners, be wild in the strike zone. I saw infielders have easy grounders go through the wickets, I saw them come off the bag, miss tags, throw wide of the bag, be handcuffed by a bad hop, and olé ground balls down the line. I saw outfielders misplay flies for triples, mistime their jump, trap sinking liners, have fly balls bounce off the heel of their glove, miss the cutoff man, airmail throws to third, and short-hop throws to the plate. I saw catchers get hit by foul tips, drop pop-ups, miss tags, drop throws, commit passed balls, and get crossed up. I saw runners get picked off first, overslide the bag at second, make the first out of the inning at third, and run through the stop sign to be out by a mile at home. I saw batters bunt foul with two strikes, miss a sign, hit a line drive into the shift, take a called third strike with men on base after being ahead in the count 3-0, swing at balls that bounce in front of the plate.

"Blessed One, you have made a game where the best batters fail to get a hit 70 percent of the time, where the scoreboard in every stadium each day displays a giant E, where a 'quality start' yields a 4.50 ERA, where relief pitchers are judged not by their wins but by their saves, the number of times they avert disaster. A team that loses four of every ten games always goes to the playoffs; a team that loses five of every ten games never does. All of this takes place in a season that seems endless, 162 games, many endured in the dog days of August. Blessed One, holding high one of my sixteen Gold Gloves, I ask you: Why did you make a game so suffused with suffering?"

The Buddha responded, "Well said, well said, Original Twin, you, who should be in the Hall of Fame. You speak the truth. I have made a game in which there are so many ways to fail, and those failures are recorded for all time, for all to see, and for all to ponder. I made this game to teach the truth of suffering.

"I teach the suffering of pain. This is the suffering known to all, the decline in a player's skills over the course of his career: the drop in bat speed for the hitter, the reduction in range for the fielder, the loss of miles per hour off the fastball for the pitcher. This is the suffering felt by each fan with each loss, felt by player and fan alike when the team does not make the playoffs. This is the suffering of player and fan alike in this game where most players have a good year among many bad years, not a bad year among many good years.

"I teach the suffering of change. This is when that which once seemed to be a source of pleasure becomes a source of pain. This is why I made a game that is long and can always be longer, where the excitement felt by fans upon entering the stadium and seeing the field of green as they make their way through the concourse turns into restlessness as the game moves into the late innings of a laugher. This is why I made a season that is so long, where the excitement of the players on Opening Day has been sapped by the trade deadline.

"I teach the suffering of conditioning, that each player on each team and each fan in each seat, and each fan watching at home and each fan listening in the car, is ready to undergo suffering in each moment. I have made a game where some three hundred pitches are thrown in each game and each of those pitches is a moment of failure for the pitcher or the hitter, for the fielder or the runner, and always for the fan of one team or the other. In order to teach the suffering of conditioning, I have

made a game in which there are so many ways to fail."
Thus spoke the Buddha.

Commentary

Buddhism is renowned for its doctrine of suffering. The
Buddha's famous statement "All is suffering" is often
heard. Suffering is the first of the four noble truths, the
subject of the Buddha's first teaching after he achieved
enlightenment. As one might expect, then, there are
detailed discussions of the nature of suffering in Buddhist texts, with much insight and nuance. The statement that "All is suffering," a statement often cited to
describe Buddhism as "pessimistic," is not a claim that
we are racked with pain during every moment of our
existence. Something more subtle is meant by the term
"suffering." Here in *The Baseball Sutra*, the Buddha al-
ludes to what he calls the three types of suffering, each
of which occurs in life, and each of which occurs in
baseball.

The first and most obvious type of suffering is called
the suffering of pain. It includes all of those experiences
that we find painful, both physically and mentally. For
players, this would include the myriad injuries they suffer during their career, all of those things that send
them to the trainer's room, to the team doctor, to the
hospital for an MRI, whether it makes them "day to

day," sends them to the ten-day injured list, ends their season, or ends their career.

The physical suffering of the fan is rarer, including stubbing your toe as you go up the steps on the way to your seat, getting hit with a foul ball, feeling nausea after eating a bad hot dog, or the discomfort of standing in a long line to use the restroom. The suffering of pain also includes mental pain. In baseball, this includes all the types of sadness that we feel over the course of a season, and over the course of our lives as players and fans, the sadness felt with every loss. Even the team with the best record in the live-ball era, the 2001 Mariners, lost 46 games that season and lost the ALCS to the Yankees, 4 games to 1. The 1962 Mets lost 120 games. But the Mets won 40 games that season, so when the Buddha says "All is suffering," he is not referring to the Mets' suffering of pain; there were moments of pleasure in that miserable season.

The second type of suffering is called the suffering of change. This is the idea, one that seems counterintuitive, that feelings of pleasure will eventually turn into feelings of pain. Buddhist texts give the example of carrying something heavy on your right shoulder. Eventually, your right shoulder will begin to hurt, so you shift the load to your left shoulder. Immediately your right shoulder feels better, but soon your left shoulder starts to hurt and you have to switch it back.

In baseball, an example would be coming out of the cold concrete concourse after a long walk to the stadium, feeling the comfort of being able to sit in one's seat in the bleachers and bask in the warm sun. But as the game progresses, the seat becomes uncomfortable and you get a headache from sitting for hours in the sun field. You have to get up and walk around the concourse to cool off and stretch your legs. Then you start to get cold, so you return to your seat. From the Buddhist perspective, most of our life involves tacking back and forth between various activities, doing what makes us feel better until it starts to make us feel worse, then doing something else.

According to conventional wisdom, pleasure and pain are two sides of the same coin. However, in Buddhism, there is a more radical claim, that pleasure and pain are different, and one of the important ways in which they differ is that a painful experience will remain painful unless one does something to stop the pain, while pleasure will eventually turn into pain unless one knows when to stop doing the thing that caused pleasure in the first place. A pitcher who feels a shooting pain in his elbow from having torn the ulnar collateral ligament will never pitch without pain until he has Tommy John surgery and rehabs for at least a year. That pain will never become pleasure. Yet pleasure will become pain. The batter who experiences the pleasure of winning the

Home Run Derby during the All-Star break will feel that pleasure turn into pain when he goes into a slump in the second half.

The third type of suffering is called the suffering of conditioning. It is the most subtle and the most pernicious. It is called the "suffering of conditioning" because our minds and bodies are so conditioned that we are susceptible to suffering at any and every moment of our existence. The suffering of conditioning is a consequence of impermanence, the fact that everything, both ourselves and the world, is changing each moment, and thus that we are susceptible to suffering in each moment because the changes that we undergo are so rarely under our control. All manner of accidents can befall us, all manner of diseases can strike us down, all manner of morbid thoughts can invade our mind. That is, although we do not undergo the suffering of pain in each moment, we are poised to undergo the suffering of pain in the next moment.

This truth is often expressed in Buddhist texts, where we read that it is a miracle that we go to sleep each night and wake up the next morning, where we read that we cannot say with certainty that we will not die in the next moment. We are constantly subject to, and subjected to, change, a change over which we have no control. In Buddhism, there is no form of suffering that is more horrific. It is this form of suffering that motivates the

Buddhist to find a state beyond this uncontrolled and uncontrollable change, a state where there is no change, a state called nirvana.

In *The Baseball Sutra*, Jim Kaat, the veteran left-hander who won twenty games three times over his long career, rises from his place in the broadcast booth. He enumerates all the forms of suffering he has witnessed over the course of his twenty-five-year career as a player and his thirty-year career as a broadcaster. He concludes his discouraging, but accurate, litany by asking the Buddha, "Why did you make a game so suffused with suffering?"

The Buddha says, "I have made a game in which there are so many ways to fail, and those failures are recorded for all time, for all to see, and for all to ponder. I made this game to teach the truth of suffering." He goes on to give examples of the suffering of pain and the suffering of change for both fans and players. He then says, "I teach the suffering of conditioning, that each player on each team and each fan in each seat, and each fan watching at home and each fan listening in the car, is ready to undergo suffering in each moment." He goes on to say that between the starters and relievers on the two teams in a given game, about three hundred pitches are thrown, and each of those pitches is an occasion for the suffering of pain, not just for one person but for many: the strike (called, swinging, or fouled off) for the batter;

the ball (just outside, a wild pitch, a bad call, or a fourth ball) for the pitcher. Any player or fan could add dozens of items to this list, were it not so painful to ponder them.

The Buddha has made a game so filled with suffering in order that we can learn about the truth of suffering from playing and watching his game. No game is so filled with suffering as baseball, sufferings that are so obvious that the Buddha does not even need to enumerate them in order for us to attest to their truth. And yet these sufferings occur in a game, a game in which, at least for the fan, the stakes are low.

As has been often noted, watching sports has its own strange psychology. Watching sports in person—at the arena, at the stadium, at the ballpark—has its own complicated psychology of the crowd, that fleeting, and precarious, feeling of community shared by densely packed thousands. Watching one's team also has its own psychology, raising a host of questions about identity and identification, questions that the Buddha will address in the next chapter of *The Baseball Sutra*.

But, in addition to the mass psychology of the stadium or the solitary devotion to the favorite team, there is a different kind of watching. I will often watch a playoff game—in baseball, football (college or pro), or basketball (college or pro)—in which I have no interest whatsoever in the outcome (although even here an allegiance can almost always be concocted for the most tenuous of reasons). Even channel surfing, I will pause to watch the conclusion of "a close game" (but never a blowout), deflecting my wife's imprecations by saying, "Just a minute. Let me see what happens."

One would never stop and watch the final minutes of a movie one had never seen before, because too much of the plot had been missed; there would be no investment in the drama. One would watch the final minutes only of a movie one already knew, like Bogart's final scene with Mary Astor in *The Maltese Falcon*, or even a scene in the middle of a film, like the taxicab scene in *On the Waterfront*. But here, one knows the outcome; the pleasure of the viewing comes not from the unexpected but from the familiar, the chance to savor once again the actor's craft and the writer's words. The random sporting event is something different. One has not seen it before; one does not know the players. And yet there is an immediate investment in the drama that compels the viewer to see what happens, watching to the end, even though the game means nothing.

Perhaps we watch games that mean nothing to us for a reason. The Buddhist suffering of conditioning, the fact that we are always susceptible to suffering, is something that we tacitly acknowledge every day. We fear change. We would not board an airplane if we were not certain that the statistical chances of its crashing were tiny. We would not undergo an operation without knowing the survival rate. Each decision we make entails a prediction about a future that we cannot know, an acknowledgment of the fact that things can go very wrong and a calculation that they will not. And in those domains of human existence where such statistics are not available, notably the domains of the heart, we pledge to love each other forever, while living in constant fear that that love might die. Unpredictable change, no matter what one might say after the fact, is something we dread, something that we devote much of our waking life trying to guard against.

This is the reason why we watch games that mean nothing to us and why we find pleasure in them. It is because they mean nothing. We allow ourselves to become absorbed for a moment in someone else's suffering of conditioning, not knowing the outcome until the final second: the Hail Mary, the three-pointer at the buzzer. Here, change is under our control, or at least under our remote control, because we know when it will end. Watching such games is vicarious but not visceral; we feel the pleasure or the pain of change, but only for an instant, soon forgotten, because we have no investment in the outcome. It is change that has no consequences.

For the baseball fan, baseball is different from other sports because the suffering of conditioning both afflicts us and teaches us with every pitch in every game of a season that extends over 162 games and six months each year. Still, even though we suffer with each pitch, the wounds are superficial. And so the Buddha created the game of baseball to provide us with a place to learn about the suffering of conditioning without really suffering from it, giving us a game that serves as a solace from the changes we fear each day, changes that can be so consequential.

5

NO SELF

Then, by the power of the Buddha, an old man rose from the upper deck along the third-base line. He wore a Yankees cap and a pinstripe jersey with the number 4. Removing his cap, he addressed the Buddha. "O, One Who Has Gone to Happiness, I have been a Yankees fan my whole life, from the time I watched the '27 Yankees as a seven-year-old boy in the old Yankee Stadium to the Yankees of today. Over the course of my life, the Yankees have been good and bad, they have won and lost. Thousands of players have worn the pinstripes, some remembered, most forgotten. Now, I am one hundred years old. When I watch a game from the stands, or on television, or listen to the radio, I sometimes ask myself, What are the Yankees? Where are the Yankees? These seem odd questions, easy to answer, and yet I am plagued with doubt. I ask the Enlightened One to enlighten me."

The Buddha replied, "You ask a wise question, O Season-Ticket Holder. I will answer your question with a question of my own. Imagine a Yankees roster on Opening Day, made up of eight position players, a backup catcher, a fourth outfielder, two utility infielders, a DH, five starters, five long relievers, a seventh-inning guy, an eighth-inning guy, and a closer. Imagine that because of pulled hamstrings, pulled groins, pulled lats, oblique strains, torn anterior cruciate ligaments, concussions from running into walls, hip pointers, hit batsmen, torn ulnar collateral ligaments, bone spurs, sore shoulders, bad knees, numb fingers, hangnails, slumps, errors, losing streaks, drug suspensions, high ERA, and low OBP, every member of the twenty-six-man Opening Day roster is placed on the injured list, sent down, traded, designated for assignment, or given his release at some point during the season. Imagine that on August 31, the day before the roster expands, not a single player from the Opening Day roster remains. My question to you, Old Man, is: Is this team on August 31 the Yankees? I answer your question by repeating your question back to you: Where are the Yankees?"

The old man said, "Lord, those Yankees are not the Yankees. They may wear the pinstripes, but they are not my team. I look for the Yankees among the players on the roster but I cannot find them." The Buddha declared, "Well said, you of many seventh-inning stretches. Let me now ask more questions, and answer them myself.

"Is Yankee Stadium the Yankees? No, for Yankee

Stadium was demolished and a new structure built on a new site. Is the franchise the Yankees? No, the franchise is something concocted by lawyers and bankers, to be bought and sold by those who may not have a single at bat. Is the logo the Yankees? No, because around the world, people wear the cap with the interlocking N and Y who do not know any of the retired numbers. Is it the memories of the fans? No, because the fans grow old and die, and their memories die with them. And so I declare, nowhere are the Yankees to be found. The Yankees do not exist. The Yankees are empty. The Yankees are not the Yankees. Therefore, they are the Yankees."

The World-Honored One continued: "You see that the householder wears the tools of ignorance, but all sentient beings, players and fans, wear the tools of ignorance each day. I made this game called baseball to teach fans, players, umpires, agents, scouts, front-office people, owners, league executives, vendors, ushers, groundskeepers, writers, and broadcasters that there is no team, there is no baseball. Baseball is emptiness. Emptiness is baseball. Baseball is not other than emptiness. Emptiness is not other than baseball.

"And why? The caster of the ball seeks the emptiness of the domain of the strike—whether inside or outside, high or low, above the knees, below the letters, on the black, catching the corner—the emptiness never tainted by wood, except for a caught foul tip. The fielder of the baseball seeks the empty space of his brother's glove, whether it be the guardian of the first square, the second square, the third square, or the guardian of the household, without short hops or airmail. The striker of the baseball seeks the empty space of the hole, the gap, down the line, the intermediate space between short and deep, the emptiness in the green grass at the foot of the mountain—to the left if the hurler falls off the mountain to the right, to the right if the hurler falls off the mountain to his left—and best of all the emptiness when the ball has gone, gone, gone beyond, gone completely beyond the wall. In emptiness, there are no Yankees."

Hearing these words, some players (from other teams) vomited blood, some players' heads split open, and fans killed themselves by jumping from the upper deck. The Buddha said, "These players and fans were not yet ready to hear the ultimate truth. But fear not—they will be reborn immediately in the pure land of Fenway Park." Thus spoke the Buddha.

Commentary

In chapter three, the Buddha set forth his famous doctrine of impermanence, that everything is in a constant state of flux, where everything we try to hold on to turns to dust in our hands. This is true not only of the various objects of our senses—the things we see, hear, smell, taste, and touch—but of our own mind and body. We are aware of the changes that our bodies undergo as we grow up and as we age. We are also aware of how our ideas, our beliefs, our tastes, our values, our likes, and our dislikes change over time.

All of this, however, is conventional wisdom, conveyed in various maxims in many cultures around the world and across the ages. All of this describes what Buddhists call coarse impermanence. There is also subtle impermanence: the constant arising and ceasing, production and destruction, the coming into existence and the going out of existence, the birth and the death of everything in each moment. And so, the Buddha teaches non-attachment, because ultimately there is nothing to be attached to. However, there is a further implication of the doctrine of impermanence, one that is the most radical of the Buddha's claims and that is considered the hallmark of Buddhist philosophy: the doctrine of no self. It is the third mark. It is the third strike.

When the idea of subtle impermanence is applied to what we call the person, it is found that all of the constituents of our body, whether solid or fluid—our bones, muscles, tendons, organs, teeth, hair, blood, sweat, and tears—are in constant flux, changing every moment. Again, we do not see this, because we are bewitched by the spell of continuity. It is also found that all of the constituents of our mind—our capacities to see, hear, smell, taste, and touch; our memories, our thoughts, and dreams—are also in constant flux, changing every moment. We do not see this because of a far more dangerous delusion: the belief in self.

If everything encompassed within these forms and feelings that we call the person is constantly changing, if nothing within the complex of mind and matter lasts longer than an instant, then where is the self, the soul, that which is most essentially me? What is it that I point to when I tap my index finger on my chest?

The Buddha's claim is that there is no self, there is no soul; there is no possessor of possessions, no doer of deeds, no thinker of thoughts; there is no someone who resides somewhere in the mind and the body. And it is the Buddha's claim that the belief in self is the most fundamental form of ignorance, and the most devastating. It is the belief in self that leads to the desires that are supposed to soothe the self and to the hatreds that are supposed to protect it. Instead, they bring only suffering in their wake, for oneself and for others.

Yet this belief in self, this most fundamental form of ignorance, is deep-seated and primeval, not easily dispelled. In Buddhism, with its doctrine that each of us has been reborn in countless forms countless times in the past, it is said that a moment of ignorance, a moment of the belief in self, serves as the first cause of each rebirth. The belief in self is the engine that drives the most pernicious perpetual motion machine, the ever-turning wheel of birth and death. The purpose of the Buddhist path, therefore, is to destroy this ignorance forever, to destroy the effect by destroying its cause. Ignorance is destroyed by wisdom, and wisdom is the gateway to nirvana.

However, this is not just the generic wisdom of the wise. It is a precise and specific knowledge—arrived at through analysis and deepened through meditation—that there is no self.

That analysis entails first identifying what it is that we call the self. It is elusive, but it is said to manifest most often as a feeling in the center of the chest, one that appears strongly in moments of great pride ("I did it!") and moments of false accusation ("I didn't do it!"). After evoking this feeling through imagining such situations, one then begins a methodical inventory of all the constituents of what we think of as the person, and asks in each case, "Is this me?"

Beginning at the feet, one can ask about each toe, each toenail, the bones of the legs, the muscles, asking in each case, "Is this me?" and answering "No," because without these, I would still be me. One moves up to the genitals, asking the same question, and arriving, perhaps after some reflection, at the same answer. Then upward to the internal organs, the kidneys, the liver, the lungs, the heart. We cannot live without these, but we can imagine a time when artificial versions can be implanted inside us, continuing to allow us both to live and to be ourselves. Moving up to the head, we arrive at four of the five sense organs—the eyes, the ears, the nose, the tongue—asking in each case whether without them we would still be ourselves. Many live without one or more of the senses, yet they maintain their personal identity.

Having surveyed the physical and not found the self, we turn to the mind, what would seem the self's likely abode. Watching the mind with the mind, we observe passing thoughts; moments of distraction replaced by moments of obsession; hopes displaced by fears; memories triggered by this song or that phrase, this scent or that color—an apparently random series of feelings, impressions, ideas, sustained for more than a moment only with particular effort. Which of these is me? The conclusion, the Buddhists claim, is that none is, that each element of the person, whether physical or mental, lasts for just an instant, only to be replaced in the next moment by another, which itself immediately fades. Within this process, there is nothing that is the owner of these body parts and those mental events. The self that seems so real is, upon analysis, merely an illusion. To the question "Where is the self," the Buddha answers, "Nowhere."

A similar question was asked by the ancient Greek author Plutarch about the ship of Theseus, the legendary founder of Athens. During his many adventures, Theseus sailed to the island of Crete, where he slew the Minotaur and followed Ariadne's thread out of the monster's labyrinth. When he returned, his ship was kept in the port of Athens as a memorial, sailed each year to the island of Delos to honor Apollo. Over the years, the wooden planks of the ship began to rot, needing to be replaced, one by one. Eventually, every piece of the ship—the planks, the oars, the masts—had been replaced. Plutarch asks the obvious question: Is this still the ship of Theseus?

The Buddhist example is similar but also different, and the question that it asks is more radical. Plutarch is asking whether the ship that was once there is still there. Plutarch assumes that a ship was there in the first place. For the Buddha, the self is an illusion; it has never existed.

A famous Buddhist philosopher of seventh-century India, named Chandrakirti, used the example of a chariot. Chariots in ancient India were similar to those of the Greeks and Romans, with a car for the driver, wheels with multiple spokes, an axle, a pole, and an apparatus to yoke the horses to the chariot. In what is known as the "sevenfold reasoning," Chandrakirti examines the logical problem of trying to find the chariot among its parts. He argues that (1) the chariot is not the same as its parts, because, since there are many parts, there would need to be many chariots; that (2) the chariot is not different from its parts, because in that case there would a chariot that existed separate from its parts; that (3) the parts do not depend on the chariot, because in that case the parts and the chariot would be two different things; that (4) the chariot does not depend on its parts, because in that case the chariot and its parts would again be two different things; that (5) the chariot does not possess its parts, because the idea of possessor and possession implies two different things; that (6) the chariot is not the collection of its parts, because if the parts were simply piled together they would not be a chariot; and (7) the chariot is not its parts assembled into a particular shape, because the shape of the parts does not change when they are assembled, and it is has already been shown that the parts are not the chariot.

There is much to ponder here, but Chandrakirti's claim is that when we subject something like a chariot to careful analysis, it cannot be found. This does not mean that chariots don't exist or that you can't ride in a chariot from one place to another. It simply means that the chariot does not exist in the way we imagine it to. The chariot is really just an idea that we project onto a collection of parts arranged in a particular way that perform a particular function. This may not seem particularly consequential, but Chandrakirti provides the analysis of the chariot as an example of how to analyze the self. Offering a more philosophical approach than the catalogue of body and mind, he argues that just as the chariot is not to be found among its parts, so the self is not to be found among the various parts of the body and the mind.

The Buddha created the game of baseball in order to teach us that there is no self, and he does it in a way that is easier to understand than the logical arguments of ancient India. The old fan who rises from his season-ticket seat explains that he has watched the Yankees for decades, making the pilgrimage to Yankee Stadium for thousands of home games over the years. During those years, he has seen hundreds of players wear the pinstripes.

In Buddhism, it is often said that profound questions are made "by the power of the Buddha"—that is, that the Buddha plants the question in the person's mind so that he may answer it. Wearing a Yankees cap and a home jersey with Lou Gehrig's retired number, the old man asks where, among all the people and things that bear the name "Yankees," the Yankees are to be found. It is a profound question. Indeed, baseball provides a perfect opportunity to ponder questions of personal identity, of self and no self. And because the Buddha's truths are eternal truths, what the Buddha will teach was also true before free agency.

As he often does, the Buddha responds to a question

with a question of his own, asking the man to imagine a season in which the entire twenty-six-man roster is replaced, one player at a time, by the time the rosters expand after August. Just as Plutarch asks whether the new ship of Theseus is the old ship of Theseus, the Buddha asks whether that team would be the Yankees. When the man says no, the Buddha asks him about a number of other things that might be the Yankees, but the old man says that none of them are the Yankees.

Baseball provides the opportunity to ponder no self because it so often causes us, both player and fan, to expand the sense of self beyond our own mind and body to the team—and not just to the team of today's game or of this season, but to the team's entire history. And when, like the Yankees, the franchise has never moved, that history is long. In baseball, fans often speak of their favorite team in the first-person plural: "2009 was the last year we won the World Series." The old fan who has watched so many games over so many seasons is troubled by this.

This sense of personal identity takes on peculiar forms in those postseasons when, as is true for most fans, their team did not make the playoffs. Some fans stop watching, but most will watch, relishing the intensity of those games in which so much rides on every pitch. Because of the deeply engrained sense of self, a strange psychology comes into play in deciding which team to root for in postseason play: each league's Wild Card Game, the League Division Series, the League Championship Series and the World Series. In each case, a complicated calculus comes into play, displaying at every round the illusion of self. This calculus is different for each person. In the interests of full disclosure, I will reveal my own.

If the Yankees are not in the playoffs, I will tend to root for the team from the Eastern Division of the American League unless that team is the Red Sox. Among these I give preference to the Orioles, because I grew up in the Washington area and Frank Robinson was one of my favorite players. However, since I have spent most of my academic career at the University of Michigan, I will also root for the Tigers. In playoffs between a Central Division team and a Western Division team, I will root for the Central Division team unless the Western Division team is the Mariners, because (at least at the time of this writing) they haven't won in a long time.

I usually don't follow the National League as closely, but in the NLDS and NLCS I root for the great teams of my youth: the Phillies, the Pirates, the Cardinals, the Dodgers, and the Giants. If any of these teams were playing against another of them, I would concoct some reason to root for one team over the other.

In the World Series, I will always root for the American League team, unless it is the Red Sox. As I write these words, all of this seems very intuitive to me. But as I read them, I can see that they are based on all manner of odd memories and largely meaningless geographical associations. The only thing that seems perfectly logical is my antipathy for the Red Sox.

This is what makes the Buddha's focus on the question of the team so potent. In Buddhism, when the idea of no self is talked about in more universal terms, expanding it beyond the person, the term "emptiness" is often used instead of "no self," meaning that everything is devoid, or empty, of any kind of essence or true nature that makes it what it is. Just as a self is not to be found in the mind and the body, a chariot is not to be found among its parts. The chariot is empty of being a chariot. As we all know, the word "team" is used to name a group, an assembly, a collection—first the starting players, but in fact the entire roster, and then the entire apparatus of coaches, trainers, grounds crew, and publicists that make it possible for the players to play the game. Where, among these parts, are the Yankees to be found?

In his sutras, the Buddha rarely speaks in the complicated language of Buddhist philosophy. His words are more cryptic, more poetic, and more evocative. And so in *The Baseball Sutra* he says, "The Yankees are empty. The Yankees are not the Yankees. Therefore, the Yankees are the Yankees." What he means is that when one looks for the Yankees among all the things that we imagine might be the Yankees, we can't find the Yankees. Therefore, the Yankees are not the Yankees. However, this absence of the Yankees does not mean that the Yankees are utterly nonexistent. In Buddhism, emptiness is not depressing, but inspiring. It is the fact that nothing exists in the way that it appears, that everything is instead just a projection by our own minds, which makes everything possible.

Consider the bases: white canvas cushions, fifteen inches square, once filled with sand or sawdust—all things of little value. Yet depending on their placement in the diamond of dirt, they take on great meaning. First is only ninety feet away, easy to reach with a walk, a hit, an error, a hit-by-pitch, a passed-ball third strike, a Baltimore chop. But it is also a place of danger from the pickoff—by taking an extra step, falling asleep, leaning toward second. Second is safer—in scoring position, able to steal signs—yet it is also a place of peril: the site of the 6-4-3 double play, the force-out, the caught-stealing, the overslide, the hidden-ball trick. Third is the destination of the triple, "the most exciting play in baseball," but the place never to make the first or third out. From third it is easy to score on a sacrifice fly, a passed ball, a safety squeeze, or a suicide squeeze, or to walk home on a walk-off. Yet third is also a place to be stranded.

These identical bags each have their own profound meaning; we need not speak of the importance of home plate. These bags of canvas are nothing in themselves, their associations projected upon them by fan, player, umpire, and coach, mentally removing the sawdust and stuffing the bags with meaning. All of the objects of our experience—the pleasing and painful, the loved and loathed—are like those bags: meaning nothing in themselves, meaning something only because we imagine that they do.

And so the Buddha says that the Yankees are not the Yankees. And because the Yankees are not the Yankees, they are the Yankees. He goes on to equate emptiness with baseball, saying, "Baseball is emptiness. Emptiness is baseball. Baseball is not other than emptiness. Emptiness is not other than baseball." Here, he explains how emptiness, empty space, is so important to the game: the empty pocket of the first baseman's mitt as he awaits the relay throw to complete the double play, the empty space down the line where so many doubles fall, the empty space beyond the wall in dead center.

The doctrine of emptiness is renowned as the most difficult and profound of the Buddha's teachings, challenging our most deeply held views of that most precious possession: our self. It is such a head-splitting doctrine that in some Buddhist texts, the heads of those who can't handle it literally split open. For others, emptiness is so viscerally powerful that they vomit blood.

This happens in Yankee Stadium, among both players and fans. However, the Buddha reassures his audience that they need not be concerned about the fate of those who have dropped dead, explaining that they will all be reborn in Fenway Park.

6

KARMA

Then a New York City firefighter rose from the stands behind home plate, took off his helmet, and addressed the Buddha. "Blessed One, I have been a Yankees fan my entire life. I lost many brothers and sisters on September 11. That year, the Yankees won the pennant and faced the Diamondbacks in the World Series. They brought great hope to the city of New York in a time of grief. They had come-from-behind victories in Games Four and Five in extra innings, with dramatic home runs by Tino, Jeter, and Brosius. They went to Arizona for Game Seven, a tense pitching duel between Schilling and the Rocket, with Alfonso Soriano, he of the mammoth bat, hitting a solo shot in the eighth to put the Yankees up 2-1. Joe called in the greatest relief pitcher in history to close out the game and bring the trophy back to New York. And yet the Yankees lost. How is this possible?"

The Buddha said, "Nothing occurs by chance. Everything is the result of our past deeds. I will tell you a story. Long ago, there were three brothers, the sons of a merchant who served the king. One day, they climbed over the wall into the king's private gardens, where he had a menagerie of wild animals that he had tamed. The king's prized possession was a king cobra. The three boys were throwing a ball back and forth as they ran laughing through the garden. Suddenly, the middle brother threw the ball to the youngest brother. But the boy missed the ball. It struck the snake, killing it.

"The boys ran away in fear, but before they could climb back over the wall, they were captured by the king's soldiers, who took them before the king and told him what had happened. The king was enraged and had the brothers locked in the dungeon, declaring that the one who threw the ball and killed the snake would be executed the next day. The oldest brother stepped forth and declared that he had thrown the ball, even though he had not. The king proclaimed that he would be beheaded at dawn.

"That night, the three boys sat together in their cell, weeping at their fate. The royal jailer was a wise old man. He unlocked the door to the dungeon and came in. He told the boys that he had seen what happened, that the boys had not meant to kill the cobra, that it was the cobra's time to die, according to the law of karma. Unlocking the window of their cell, he told the boys to escape.

"The two younger brothers immediately jumped out

and ran home, but the oldest brother remained. He asked the old jailer, 'What will happen to you?' The jailer said that the next day, after the boys were safely home, he would go before the king, admit what he had done, and take his own life, standing at the foot of the throne. The boy refused to go, saying that he would not allow him to make such a sacrifice. But the jailer explained that he was an old man and had lived a good life. He was happy to give his life for an innocent child. The jailer again unlocked the window to the cell and held it open, telling the boy to go.

"In this lifetime, Scott Brosius was the older brother, Mariano Rivera was the middle brother, Derek Jeter was the youngest brother, and George Steinbrenner was the king. Because in a past life Mo had killed the serpent of the king, he suffered the consequences of his deed. Thus, when Damian Miller bunted to move the pinch runner over, Mo, instead of throwing a fastball to Jeter, threw a cutter that tailed away and into the outfield. Then, when Jay Bell laid down a sacrifice bunt to move the runner to third, Mo threw to Scott Brosius for the putout.

"Yet, Brosius did not throw to first for the double play, although Bell was old and a slow runner. Instead, he held the ball. And why? Because in that lifetime long ago, Jay Bell had been the old jailer of the king, who saved the lives of the three brothers. Scott Brosius does not remember his past lives. And yet, compelled by his past karma and the debt he owed to the old man, he held the ball. This in turn led to Gonzalez's broken-bat bloop over the drawn-in infield, allowing Jay Bell to score the winning run. And so the serpents won the series. Luis Gonzalez had been the snake. Scott Brosius bears no blame." Thus spoke the Buddha.

Commentary

How do we explain the inexplicable? Why do things go wrong? Why do the evil prosper? Why does suffering befall the good? These are questions that humans have pondered since the beginning of time and that all religions seek to answer. For the theistic religions, such things are often said to be the will of God, unknowable by mere mortals. In Buddhism, there is no creator God who blesses the virtuous and damns the sinful. There is, instead, the inexorable law of karma. As discussed in chapter three, the Sanskrit word *karma* simply means "action" or "deed," but in both Hinduism and Buddhism it takes on a more specific meaning, referring to a kind of natural law of the universe in which virtuous deeds cause happiness in the future and evil deeds cause suffering in the future.

In Buddhism, it is said that everything that happens to us in each of our innumerable lifetimes in the past, individually and collectively, is the result of our past deeds: whether we are reborn as a human or an animal, in heaven or in hell—if a human, our birthplace, our parents, our gender, our appearance, and our intelligence; if an animal, our species, and whether we are predator or prey.

This "law of karma," as it is sometimes called, thus explains everything about the present, but it does not allow us to predict the future. This is because we have no control over which deed from among the infinite deeds we have performed in the past will create what will befall us in the next moment. The experience of the next moment may be caused by something we did yesterday or by something we did eons ago. In many ways, it is a doctrine of individual responsibility, allowing us to take the credit for our fortune and forcing us to take the blame for our failure—but only in a general sense, because exactly what we did when to cause us happiness or despair is unknown to the unenlightened.

It is said that on the night of his enlightenment, the Buddha had a vision of all of his past lives, remembering each of them—although they were infinite in number—in specific detail. It is also said that the Buddha knows the past deeds of all the beings in the universe, allowing him to identify the deeds done in the past that explain why something has happened in the present. And because he knows how the seeds of past deeds will fructify, he can also predict the future.

One of the most popular forms of Buddhist literature is the so-called birth stories, in which the Buddha recounts events from his past lives, sometimes as a human and sometimes as an animal. In these stories, the future Buddha is the protagonist, often a generous king or a brave animal who sacrifices his own welfare for others. The Buddha's own disciples are often characters in the story, demonstrating their long karmic connection to the Buddha. The Buddha's evil cousin, who attempted to assassinate him, is usually the villain, his antagonism born out of many lifetimes of envy and jealousy.

Baseball fans, like all humans, ask why there is evil in the world and why the innocent suffer. But they ask additional questions of equal profundity: What would Ted Williams' career numbers have been if he did not lose almost five seasons to the Marines during the peak of his skills? What would Mickey Mantle's career totals have been if his spikes hadn't gotten caught in a drainage grate in right field in Yankee Stadium in the second game of the 1951 World Series? How many RBIs would Lou Gehrig have had if he hadn't gotten sick? What would have happened if Moisés Alou had caught that foul fly ball in Game Six of the 2003 NLCS? What would have happened if the great Bill Buckner had fielded that slow roller to first in 1986?

For Yankee fans, Mantle's injury-free career remains the perennial question to ponder. But in the current century, no question looms larger than this: How did the Yankees lose Game Seven of the 2001 World Series?

From the Buddhist perspective, every event is fated to be; there is no point in agonizing over what might have been. And yet we do. Only the Buddha knows the events that led to that heartbreaking disaster. Out of his infinite compassion, he reveals the answer in *The Baseball Sutra*.

Before describing what happened in the misty past, it is useful to recount the painful events of 2001, for the sake of readers who are not Yankee fans and thus do not remember every moment. It is important to recall first that it was in the 2001 ALDS that the Yankees, down two games to none to the A's in the best-of-five series, won Game Three 1-0 on a solo home run by Jorge Posada and a brilliantly pitched shutout by Mike Mussina, closed out by Rivera. It was during this game that the most famous play in recent memory occurred: Derek Jeter's corralling of Shane Spencer's errant throw to the cutoff man and his shovel pass to Posada to tag out Jeremy Giambi (who did not slide) in the bottom of the seventh. In the ALCS, Yankees easily defeated the Mariners in five games, despite Seattle's having won a staggering 116 games during the regular season.

The Yankees had won the three previous World Series, and now sought their fourth straight world championship against the Arizona Diamondbacks. They lost the first two games in Phoenix before returning to Yankee Stadium, where Roger Clemens won Game Three, giving up only one run (on a sacrifice fly) over seven innings, with Rivera closing out the game.

Games Four and Five were among the most memorable in recent Yankee history. In Game Four, the Yankees were down 3-1, with two outs in the bottom of the ninth and Paul O'Neill on first, when Tino Martinez hit the first pitch out, tying the game. It was almost midnight, my wife was asleep, and I remember leaping up and emitting a Munch-esque silent scream of joy. Then, in the bottom of the tenth, the calendar having turned to November, Jeter hit a home run over the short porch to win the game.

The next night had equally heart-stopping heroics, with another two-out, bottom-of-the-ninth, game-tying home run, this time by Scott Brosius. Then Soriano drove in Knoblauch in the bottom of the twelfth to end the game, sending the series back to Arizona, with the Yankees up three games to two. The Yankees were ready to close out the series in Game 6 behind their playoff stalwart Andy Pettitte, but they were crushed 15-2; Yankee fans remain convinced that Pettitte was tipping his pitches.

The stage was set for Game 7. It was Clemens against Schilling, with Schilling pitching on three days' rest for the second time in the series. The game was tied 1-1 in the top of the eighth when Soriano hit a towering home run to left to give the Yankees the lead. Randy Johnson, who had thrown 104 pitches the night before, came on in relief, holding the Yankees scoreless. Rivera came in to pitch the bottom of the eighth, striking out the side. He returned for the bottom of the ninth, the Yankees leading 2-1, ready to close out the series.

Former Cub great Mark Grace opened with a single up the middle. He was lifted for a pinch runner. Man on first, no one out. Damian Miller bunted, as expected, right in front of the mound. Rivera, an excellent fielder, whirled to throw out the lead runner at second, where Jeter was covering. Although he seemed to have time, the ball tailed high and to the right, just out of Jeter's reach and into center. Men on first and second, no one out.

The thirty-five-year-old veteran Jay Bell was up next. Everyone knew he would bunt, to third if he could, making Brosius field the ball and allowing the pinch runner to move to third with one out. Bell bunted sharply toward third, but Rivera pounced on the ball and threw to Brosius for the force. Brosius held the ball. The all-seeing Tim McCarver, calling the game, immediately noted that Brosius could have thrown the slow-footed Bell out at first for the double play. This was confirmed by an overhead shot of the diamond, showing Bell only halfway down the line when Brosius caught the ball and Tino Martinez already at the bag, covering first.

Tony Womack followed with a double down the right field line. The game was tied 2-2, still only one out. Craig Counsell, with hands held high, was up next. Rivera plunked him to load the bases. With the infield drawn in, Gonzalez hit his broken-bat bloop, scoring Jay Bell with the winning run.

How could this have happened? Fielders make errors, both errors of commission and errors of omission. Hitters get clutch hits. But for all manner of cosmic reasons, the Yankees seemed fated to win the game, and to win the World Series. They had the greatest relief pitcher in the history of baseball on the mound, they had a future Hall of Famer at short, and they had the rock-solid MVP of the 1998 World Series and Gold Glove winner at third. During the 2000 regular season, Rivera had seven wins and thirty-six saves. In seventy-five and two-thirds innings pitched, he had not committed a single error. And yet Rivera threw the ball into center. And yet Brosius held the ball. And yet the Yankees lost. There must be an explanation.

For Buddhists, the explanation lies in the law of karma. Mariano Rivera, Derek Jeter, Scott Brosius, and Jay Bell did something in a past life that resulted in these events. And because they were intimately tied to each other in the bottom of the ninth at Bank One Ball-park in Phoenix, Arizona, on the night of November 4, 2001, they must have been intimately tied together in the past. Only the Buddha knows.

According to Buddhist doctrine, we have all been reborn countless times in the past. This not only means that we have been reborn everywhere in the universe and that we have been every type of being, it means that we have been in every possible relationship with every-one else. Every being in the universe—every human, every animal, every insect, every god, every ghost—has been our mother, father, and child. Every being in the universe has saved our life and taken our life. Every be-ing in the universe has given to us and stolen from us. Every being in the universe has been our best friend and our worst enemy.

This idea has profound implications for our interac-tions with others and figures prominently in many Bud-dhist teachings. It is said that we should not divide the world into friends, enemies, and those to whom we are indifferent based merely on the experiences of this sin-gle short lifetime, because the friend of this life was the enemy of a previous life, the enemy was the friend, and the person whom we pass on the street was someone we loved. It is said that we should dedicate ourselves to the welfare of others, because each of those others has been our mother, in fact our human mother, in a past life. The

Buddha added free agency to the game of baseball in order to teach this truth, teaching us that friends become enemies, enemies become friends, teammates become opponents, and opponents become teammates, not just from lifetime to lifetime but from season to season, and even within a single season.

The doctrine of karma and rebirth is also used to explain the present and predict the future by recounting the past. What happened in the past to cause what happened in the present? How will what we do in the present unfold in the future? This is something that only the Buddha knows, and entire genres of Buddhist literature are devoted to the stories that he tells. The story often begins with a question from one of his disciples, asking him to explain an otherwise inexplicable situation. And so in *The Baseball Sutra*, a New York City firefighter rises in the stands and asks the Buddha how the Yankees could have lost Game 7, and the Buddha tells the story.

Like most of the stories, it takes place in ancient India. Three young boys, all brothers, climb over a wall into the pleasure garden of the king, running around and playing, throwing a ball back and forth. When the middle brother throws the ball to the youngest brother, the ball accidentally hits the king's prized pet snake, killing it. The boys are caught and dragged before the king, who proclaims that the boy who killed the snake must die. The older brother immediately confesses to killing the snake, although he had not thrown the ball. The boys are tossed into prison for the night, the oldest brother to be executed at dawn.

The old jailer knows what happened—that the death of the snake had been an accident, that the oldest brother was innocent. He thus helps the boys escape through a window. The two youngest boys run to safety, but the oldest brother remains behind, asking the guard, "What will happen to you for letting us escape?" The jailer says that the next day, after the boys are safely home, he will go before the king, admit what he has done, and take his own life, standing at the foot of the throne. The boy refuses to go, saying that he will not allow him to make such a sacrifice, but the jailer explains that he is an old man and is ready to die. He holds open the heavy iron grate to the window of the dungeon, allowing the oldest brother to escape.

The Buddha explains that the oldest brother was Scott Brosius, the middle brother was Mariano Rivera, Derek Jeter was the youngest brother, George Steinbrenner was the king, and Jay Bell was the jailer. In Buddhism, intention is of great importance, the intention behind a deed figuring strongly in the karmic effect of that deed in the future. There is a certain justice to the law of karma. The jailer knew that the killing of the snake had been an accident and that it was unjust that a boy should die for what he did not intend to do. He therefore saved the boy's life, even though it meant giving up his own. Despite the importance of intention, in Buddhist literature there also stories of the future consequences of unintentional deeds, of karmic debts that still must be repaid.

Jeter and Mo had to suffer the consequences of killing the snake, even though it was an accident. But more important, Scott Brosius had to repay Jay Bell for sparing his life in a lifetime long ago, a lifetime that neither of them remembered. Thus, when Jay Bell laid down a sacrifice bunt in front of the mound and Rivera fielded the ball cleanly and threw a strike to third for the putout, something deep in the psyche of Scott Brosius caused him to hold the ball, rather than throw it to Tino Martinez at first for the twin killing. After Tony Womack doubled in the tying run, Jay Bell stood at third. Luis Gonzalez, who had been the king's pet snake in that previous life, blooped the ball over the drawn-in Derek Jeter, allowing Jay Bell to run home to win the game and the Series.

7

VAJRAPANI

Then Pudge Fisk, Son of the Sox, the red and the white, rose from his place at the household, adjusted his chest protector, and said, "Lord, long ago, in Fenway Park, the Splendid Splinter rode in a chariot to the middle of the mandala, surrounded by ninety-nine gods of the past century and all the All-Stars of the season. He turned to Big Mac and said, 'Son of St. Louis, when you foul one back, have you ever smelled smoke?' Lord, I was there that night and I heard those words, but I did not understand. What was the meaning of those words?"

The Buddha replied, "Son of the Sox, Teddy Ball-game spoke in the twi-night language, understood by only the initiates of the secret signs. He spoke of the esoteric teaching, revealed to few." He then was silent.

Soon the sound of a bat being taken from the bat rack was heard from the visitors' dugout. Ted Williams, tall and thin, The Kid of the 1941 season, as if cryogenically preserved, emerged from the dugout, walked to the on-deck circle, rubbed his bat with a bone, and knelt on one knee. The crowd roared, but Williams did not tip his cap. The Buddha then spoke, "O Last Man to Bat .400. Reveal your true nature."

At that time, The Thumper rose, holding his bat in his left hand. Suddenly he was enveloped by a blinding light, brighter than a billion night-game bulbs. From the light emerged a wrathful deity, dark blue in color, wreathed in flames, wearing a triple crown, a vajra held aloft in his left hand, striking fear into the hearts of the *Boston Globe* writers. The fans cringed in their seats; the players hid behind their gloves.

The Buddha said, "Fear not, children of good slugging percentage. Behold the bodhisattva Vajrapani. He has been worshiped for centuries across the continent of Asia, from the peaks of Tibet to the islands of Japan, as the bodhisattva of power—indeed, the embodiment of all the power of all the buddhas of the three times. He holds in his hand the vajra, this word difficult to understand by those of the Western continents, some calling it a diamond scepter, some calling it a thunderbolt.

"But these scholars of my teaching speak from ignorance. For if they were to see the most ancient rock carvings of my deeds—my birth, my enlightenment, my turning of the wheel of the dharma—they would see a mysterious figure to my left, holding a club in his left hand. This is the true Vajrapani. And today I reveal the true meaning of his name. 'Vajra' does not mean 'diamond scepter' or 'thunderbolt' or all the names one reads in books by those who call themselves scholars of Buddhism. The Sanskrit *vajra* means 'bat.' The Sanskrit word *pani* means 'hand.' 'Vajrapani' means 'one who holds the bat.' 'Vajrapani' means 'batter.'

"Some say that the game of baseball was invented by Abner Doubleday in America in 1839. This is the view of the benighted. Some say that the game of baseball was invented in England more than a century earlier. This is the view of the shortsighted. Archaeologists who excavate the ancient depictions of my deeds will see Vajrapani by my side, bat resting on his left shoulder, in carvings that are two thousand years old. I invented the game of baseball to teach the dharma, never teaching without my best batter by my side, just as the Old Professor never played a game without his man. All the buddhas of the past, all the buddhas of the present, and all the buddhas of the future create the game of baseball in age after age so that all beings, players and fans alike, can pass beyond sorrow.

"And in season after season, Vajrapani appears in uniform, bat in hand, from the Little Leagues, to Low A, to the majors, striking fear into the hearts of opposing pitchers. In the time of wars, Vajrapani appeared in the world as Ted Williams. And yet, over all these seasons, he has not revealed the secret teaching. There goes Vajrapani, the greatest hitter who ever lived." Thus spoke the Buddha.

Commentary

In Buddhism, there is the figure called the *bodhisattva*, a term that means something like "one who aspires to enlightenment." This is slightly misleading, because it would seem that in Buddhism everyone is supposed to aspire to enlightenment. Here, however, "enlightenment" (*bodhi* in Sanskrit) means Buddhahood, a state considered to be loftier and more difficult to attain than nirvana. A bodhisattva, therefore, is someone who could attain the more accessible state of nirvana rather easily, perhaps even in this very lifetime, but who instead vows to achieve the more distant state of Buddhahood, embarking on a long path that takes billions of lifetimes to complete. Bodhisattvas undertake this journey because of their compassion for the world, each seeking to become a Buddha in the future and at a time and a place where the teachings of the Buddha are not known, revealing the path that leads to liberation from the cycle of birth and death.

The path of the bodhisattva is long, in part because in order to achieve Buddhahood, the bodhisattva must accumulate great merit. Merit in Buddhism is the power that comes from performing all manner of virtuous deeds for the sake of others. Merit is essentially good karma, which will someday fructify in the form of the many wondrous qualities of the Buddha, including his knowledge of the past, present, and future, both his own and that of all beings. The virtues that the bodhisattva practices over the course of so many lifetimes are enumerated in different ways. In one famous system, there are ten, one practiced on each of ten ascending levels, or stages, on the path to Buddhahood, virtues like generosity, patience, effort, and concentration. Another of those virtues is power.

As Buddhism developed in India, certain advanced bodhisattvas became very famous, depicted often in paintings and statues. Three were particularly important, each said to embody one of three qualities of a Buddha: wisdom, compassion, and power. The Buddhist faithful appeal to the bodhisattva of compassion to rescue them from danger, they appeal to the bodhisattva of wisdom to help them dispel misconception and ignorance, and they appeal to the bodhisattva of power to defeat the forces of evil. He is Vajrapani, the wrathful bodhisattva.

Historians of ancient Indian art have been able to trace the evolution of the depiction of Vajrapani over the centuries, and scholars of Buddhist literature have been able to trace his increasing importance. In a famous early story, a proud young Hindu priest goes to see the Buddha to determine whether what he had heard about him was true. The Buddha politely invites him in and offers him a seat, but the young priest rather rudely remains standing and quizzes him about his background, making disparaging remarks about the Buddha's caste and family. When the Buddha attempts to engage him in conversation, asking him a question, he refuses to respond. The Buddha asks the question again, and still he remains silent. The Buddha tells him that he will ask him the question again, and that if he refuses to answer this third time, his head will split into seven pieces. The priest is skeptical until Vajrapani suddenly appears at the Buddha's side, carrying a flaming club; he is visible only to the Buddha and the priest. The priest says, "Could you repeat the question?"

In early Buddhist sculpture from ancient India, Vajrapani is often depicted standing next to the Buddha holding a club in his left hand. This club is called a *vajra*. Scholars have debated exactly what this term means. Sometimes it seems to be some kind of discus that is used as a weapon, sometimes it means a bolt of lightning, and sometimes it simply means something that is indestructible, like a diamond. But in dozens of early Buddhist works of art, the vajra is clearly a club, a cudgel. The word *pani* means "hand" in Sanskrit, so "Vajrapani" literally means "club-hand"—that is, "he who carries a club in his hand."

As Buddhism evolved, Vajrapani became more and

more important—no longer simply the Buddha's body-guard, but a bodhisattva in his own right: the bodhisattva of power. Buddhist deities are sometimes described as being either peaceful or wrathful, with the peaceful often depicted, like the Buddha, seated in the meditative posture, their faces serene, their hands either folded in their lap or holding the stem of a lotus flower. The wrathful deities are truly horrific, looking like monsters, often standing or dancing on the bodies of their defeated foes, a garland of skulls around their neck, brandishing all manner of weapons, often with multiple arms, their bodies wreathed in flames.

These wrathful figures challenge our stereotypes about Buddhism as a religion of peace and nonviolence, but they are on our side, working for our benefit, providing us protection. They are often bodhisattvas. And the most famous of the wrathful bodhisattvas is Vajra-pani. He becomes especially important in the tantric teachings of India and Tibet, where he reveals esoteric instructions, where it is said that bodhisattvas take on wrathful forms to destroy enemies like pride, jealousy, and hatred, their frightful visage appropriate for the de-generate age in which we live.

Buddhas and bodhisattvas appear in the world in disguise in order to benefit beings. It is said that a Bud-dha may appear as a musician or an artist, as a bridge, a breeze, or an inspiring passage in a book. Bodhisattvas

also appear in human form; Tibetan Buddhists believe
that the Dalai Lama is the human incarnation of the
bodhisattva of compassion. In *The Baseball Sutra*, the
Buddha reveals that the true meaning of the name
"Vajrapani" is not "he who holds a club," but rather "he
who holds a bat." "Vajrapani" means "batter." He reveals
also that this bodhisattva appears in the human world as
a great hitter. He further reveals that one of the human
incarnations of Vajrapani was Ted Williams.

Ted Williams was not a five-tool player. He pos-
sessed only two—he could hit and he could hit with
power. He was an average fielder, had an average arm,
and was a slow runner, something he often pointed out,
saying that his lifetime average would have been higher
if he had been able to beat out more base hits. He was,
above all, a batter, and his transcendent prowess in this
domain is beyond dispute, well known to even the most
casual fan: the last man to hit .400, two-time winner of
the Triple Crown, the highest career on-base percentage
in baseball history, winning the batting title for the fifth
and sixth times at age thirty-nine and age forty, batting
.388 when he was thirty-nine. And all this was achieved
with almost five seasons of his peak years lost to war.

For Yankee fans, the perennial question is what
Mickey Mantle's numbers would have looked like if he
hadn't been injured. For Red Sox fans, the perennial
question is what Ted Williams' number would have been

if he had not served in the Marines in both World War Two and the Korean War. Mantle's numbers are hard to project because of the variety and frequency of his injuries over his career. Williams' absence from the batter's box occurred in two specific periods (1943–45 and 1952–53), each bracketed by mostly full-time play (he broke his left arm running into the wall in 1950 and played in only eighty-nine games that year). This makes his numbers easier to plausibly project. Many such projections have been made, with most concluding that had he not had to serve, he would have hit 663 home runs and would today be the all-time leader in RBIs, ahead of Aaron and Ruth.

If "Vajrapani" means "batter," then Ted Williams was Vajrapani. This is something that I must acknowledge, even as a Yankees fan. His home runs, runs batted in, and slugging percentage all make it clear that he had tremendous power, as one would expect of the bodhisattva of power. He also had great wisdom; he was renowned for his careful analysis of his swing and his scientific approach to hitting, recorded in his 1970 book, appropriately called *The Science of Hitting*, a sacred scripture for generations of batters.

He wrote the book while he was managing the Washington Senators. He was not a particularly successful manager, never finding any rapport with the pitching staff because of the deep antipathy he felt for all pitchers. Since as a player he had the most trouble with the slider, he advised his pitchers to throw sliders. His reasoning was that if the greatest hitter of all time has trouble with the slider, all hitters must have trouble with the slider. As one might imagine, he was a more successful manager with the offense. As proof, in *The Science of Hitting* he provides a chart that shows the rising batting average of the Senators' starting lineup during his tenure at the helm.

However, a bodhisattva must have three qualities: wisdom, power, and compassion. Ted Williams was a notoriously unpleasant person, quick to anger and profane of speech. He spit at fans. He hated writers and writers hated him, so much so that one writer left him entirely off the Most Valuable Player ballot in 1947, the second time he won the Triple Crown. When he got off to a slow start in the 1940 season and was booed by the Fenway fans, he vowed never again to tip his cap, a vow that he kept for twenty years.

In the final at bat of his career in 1960, he hit a home run but did not tip his cap to acknowledge the cheering crowd at Fenway Park. Over his objections, Boston manager Mike Higgins sent him onto the field in the top of the ninth so that he could be replaced and be cheered again by the standing Fenway faithful as he left the field of play for the last time. As he ran past Pumpsie Green, who was replacing him in left, he said, "Isn't this a crock of shit?" Williams jogged into the dugout, his head down. He did not reemerge.

But Ted Williams had compassion. It was simply that he reserved it for those who needed it most: dying children. Throughout his life, he donated generously to the Jimmy Fund (named after a twelve-year-old fan who had lymphoma) and encouraged others to do so. He spent countless hours at Boston hospitals with children suffering from cancer, often anonymously paying the bills for the parents. He refused to be photographed during these visits, demanding that his time with the children be kept secret. One of Vajrapani's names is Guhyapati: "Lord of Secrets."

Wisdom (about hitting), compassion (for children), and power (to right field)—these were the qualities of this bodhisattva of baseball. However, in the off-season, Ted Williams loved nothing more than hunting and fishing. He is the only baseball player in history to be a member of both the Baseball Hall of Fame and the International Game Fishing Association Hall of Fame.

But even this does not disqualify him from the rank of bodhisattva. In Buddhism, the killing of animals accrues much negative karma. Yet among the tantric saints, all considered to be bodhisattvas, there was one who subsisted entirely on fish—indeed, fish guts. Another was a fisherman who was swallowed by a fish and practiced meditation in its belly. And the most famous of all was seen one day grabbing fish from a barrel, snapping his fingers, holding them over a fire, and eating them. Such were his powers that by snapping his fingers, he was sending them to a higher rebirth before eating them. The Lord of Secrets.

In *The Baseball Sutra*, as we have seen, the Buddha declares, "And in season after season, Vajrapani appears in uniform, bat in hand, from the Little Leagues, to Low A, to the majors, striking fear into the hearts of opposing pitchers." However, the Buddha names only one of the incarnations of Vajrapani: Ted Williams. Each fan should ponder what other forms the bodhisattva of power has taken across the diamonds and across the seasons.

In 1999, Major League Baseball had fans vote for the "All-Century Team," to be introduced at the All-Star Game, played at Fenway Park that year. After all the other players had been introduced, both the All-Century Team and that year's All-Stars, a door opened in right field and a golf cart drove out, carrying Ted Williams, introduced by the public address announcer as "the greatest hitter who ever lived." He was eighty years old and very frail, barely able to stand as, held up by Tony Gwynn, he threw out the first pitch (to Red Sox immortal Carlton Fisk). The golf cart stopped at the mound and the All-Stars, past and present, gathered around to shake his hand. In the video of the event, when Mark McGwire approaches, you can hear Williams ask him whether he ever smelled smoke when he fouled one back.

8

THE SECRET TEACHING

Then a fan rose from her seat in the second deck above the short porch near the foul pole, put down her popcorn, put on her glove, and said this to the World-Honored One: "Lord, this game that you have made for us is excellent, profound, filled with many meanings, able to captivate the hearts of those of many worlds and many eras, the old and the young, the wise and the foolish. But Lord, this game that you have made is also boring, filled with moments of dead time more numerous than the grains of sand of all the beaches in Florida. We must endure endless trips to the mound, where pitcher and catcher place their gloves over their faces; we must endure the pitcher shaking off signs and stepping off the rubber, the batter stepping out of the box after each pitch to adjust his batting gloves; we must endure interminable replay reviews of plays we can clearly see with our own eyes. And we must endure the tedious time between innings, when at home we must stare at commercials for Viagra and beer and in the stands we must watch silly races of people dressed as hot dogs and watch ourselves doing embarrassing dances on the Jumbotron. And I will not speak of rain delays.

"I find no fault with the Blessed One. I know that everything he teaches is for the welfare of the fans, for the happiness of the fans, out of compassion for the teams, for the benefit, the welfare, and the happiness of players and fans. And so, holding a foul ball in my glove, I reverently ask the Enlightened One: Why did the Omniscient One make the game so boring?"

From right field, The Hammer spoke, saying, "Lord, outfielders are also bored as we stand waiting for the reliever to finish his warm-ups." From shortstop, the Wizard of Oz spoke, saying, "Lord, infielders are also bored as we stand on our toes, awaiting the pitch, and the pitcher shakes off the sign." From first base, Boog Powell spoke, saying, "Lord, first basemen are also bored, hoping that a batter gets hit by a pitch so that we have someone to talk to." From the bullpen, Goose Gossage spoke, saying, "Lord, relievers are also bored, sitting all game beyond the outfield fence, waiting to see if the game will be a blowout or a squeaker, waiting for the call from the pitching coach to start warming up." From the home dugout, Thurman Munson spoke, saying, "Lord, at the bottom of the inning, the players are also bored, waiting for our turn to bat only four times in a game." From the visitors' dugout, Edgar Martinez spoke, saying, "Lord, designated hitters are also bored, sitting on the bench all game, waiting to be able to bat when their spot in the lineup comes up." From the visitors' dugout, Smoky Burgess spoke, saying, "Lord, pinch hitters and backup catchers are also bored, waiting all game to see if we might have one at bat or play the field for one inning. And so, we reverently ask the Enlightened One: Why did the Omniscient One make the game so boring?"

The Buddha replied, "I made the game boring because life is also boring. I made the game like life, so that my disciples can learn to deal with boredom and to use boredom as a time to contemplate the nature of reality. Yet I also make the game boring to give my disciples, both players and fans, the time to practice the secret teaching that bestows great bliss."

Then, Ted Williams, moving to the plate, took his practice swings and said, "Long ago, the Blessed One taught me the secret teaching. By practicing the secret teaching, I batted .406 in 1941, going six for eight in the final doubleheader of the season on the road in Philadelphia. Lord, please reveal the goddamn secret teaching."

The Buddha said, "Well said, you with a lifetime OBP of .482. I now reveal the secret teaching, taught only to my most beloved disciples. It can be practiced in the dugout, it can be practiced in the on-deck circle, it can be practiced in the hotel instead of playing video games, it can be practiced in the off-season. Fans can practice it in the stands between innings and during a pitching change, they can practice it at home while watching a game with the sound muted, they can practice it in the off-season. It is the secret teaching of the bodhisattva Vajrapani, who has appeared in lifetime after lifetime, in season after season, as a professional hitter.

"For this secret teaching, one need not sit in the lotus posture. You may practice the secret teaching sitting in the stands or sitting in the dugout or sitting in the bullpen, or sitting at home in front of the television. Sit upright, with your spine straight and your shoulders level. Rest your hands in your lap, holding a baseball, your thumbs touching it at the top. Watch an inning of the game without speaking and without looking at your phone, absorbed in each pitch, just watching the action. Do not impede the baseball thoughts that arise in your mind—thoughts of what pitch should be thrown, which base to throw to, whether to take the extra base. Follow the ball as it moves around the field, from the rubber to the plate, from the bat to the warning track. Allow all baseball thoughts to flow, watching them, feeling the joy and the sorrow.

"Now, begin the main practice. In the middle of your torso, four finger breadths below your navel, imagine a tiny home plate, the size of a lentil bean, standing upright, its point pointing downward. Standing at that plate, imagine yourself as the wrathful bodhisattva of power, Vajrapani, but in the form of your favorite hitter of all time, dressed in the home uniform, to the right of the plate if right-handed, to the left of the plate if left-handed. You hold in your hand a Louisville Slugger of the finest white ash. As you take your practice swings, you point the bat upward, toward the top of your head. It is the bottom of the ninth of Game Seven of the World Series. Your team is down by a run. There are two outs and a runner is on second.

"As you sit in the posture, at the center of your chest imagine a tiny baseball, made of white horsehide with one hundred and eight red stitches, the ball the size of a mustard seed. As you step into the batter's box, concentrate all of your attention on your bat, confident that you are about to get hot, so hot that your bat begins to feel warm in your hands, as if it is ready to burst into flame. As you take your stance, the mantra 'Play ball' resounds through your mind.

"Now shift your focus to the tiny baseball in the center of your heart. It begins to descend through your body and toward the plate. Although it is a fastball, imagine it moving slowly, almost in slow motion. It is center cut, you see it well, you start your swing. As the bat strikes the ball on the sweet spot, imagine that you smell smoke. You get it all. Before running the bases, you drop your bat without flipping it and watch the ball travel toward deepest center field.

"Although the exit velocity is 120 mph, imagine the ball rising slowly, almost in slow motion. It travels straight up through your body, going beyond your navel, going beyond your heart, going completely beyond your throat, moving through your skull. As it moves upward you experience deeper and deeper feelings of joy, until the ball reaches the crown of your head, where it is caught by a child in the center field bleachers. Feel the bliss of the child, hear the roar of the crowd. Focusing on the tiny ball at the crown of your head, rest in bliss." Thus spoke the Buddha.

Commentary

In this chapter, the Buddha reveals the secret teaching. In Buddhism, a secret teaching is something so profound that is not disclosed to those who would not be able to understand it or who might misuse it in a way that causes them harm. A teaching is also called secret because it is stated in such a way that its meaning is not clear to those who have not been told how to interpret its words. The secret teachings of Buddhism are especially associated with tantra, regarded as a rapid path to enlightenment for those who seek to reach the state of Buddhahood quickly, not because they are unwilling or unable to traverse the long path of many lifetimes, but because their compassion is so great that they are in a great hurry to save others from the sufferings of the universe as only a Buddha is able to do.

In the popular imagination, tantra connotes sex. This is not entirely wrong, but a more accurate way to describe tantra, especially in Buddhism, is that tantra places a special emphasis on the human body. In the earliest Buddhist teachings, rebirth as a human is extolled as the best form for achieving enlightenment. Free of the intoxicating pleasures of the gods and the paralyzing pains of the denizens of hell, a human is most able to make progress on the path to enlightenment. At the same time, the human body is disparaged, with monks and nuns shaving their heads and sometimes their eyebrows, monks shaving their beards, and both wrapping their bodies in simple robes meant to hide all signs of gender. Monks and nuns take vows of celibacy, and breaking that vow entails permanent expulsion from the monastic order.

Attachment to the human body, either one's own body or the body of another, is regarded as one of the most powerful impediments to enlightenment, and all manner of meditation techniques are set forth in order to overcome that attachment. Meditation on impermanence, as described in chapter three, is a common technique, seeing the body as merely a constantly changing process of disintegration, with nothing there to hold on to.

However, there are also more graphic techniques, set forth in disgusting detail, describing the human body as a sack of filth enclosed under a thin and fragile layer of skin, describing what happens to the most delicious and expensive food as it makes its way past the lips and through the body, and describing in gruesome detail the many stages in the decay of a corpse, from what appears to be someone sleeping to the bones of a skeleton scattered in a charnel ground. The body is to be constantly restrained, sustained by alms placed in a begging bowl and protected by robes made from the shrouds of the dead. The body is therefore to be valued only as the imperfect seat of the mind, a mind that is to be used to recognize the body, and everything else, as impermanent, suffering, and not self.

Buddhist tantra presents a very different view. The body is again the seat of the mind, but it is also the essential vehicle to Buddhahood. This is not just a metaphor. It is based on a detailed tantric physiology. It is an ancient physiology, unknown to modern science. In this system, there is a network of channels that runs throughout the body. Through these channels run energies, called "winds." The movement of these winds through the channels functions like the autonomic nervous system, providing for such things as motion, digestion, and respiration.

In this network of channels, three are the most important, called simply the central channel, the right channel, and the left channel, with the central channel, about the thickness of an arrow, running from the genitals up to the crown of the head, then curving down and ending at the point between the eyes. Located along the central channel are the famous *chakras*, literally "wheels" in Sanskrit, described as networks of various smaller channels that radiate through the body. There are seven of these wheels: at the forehead, the crown of the head, the throat, the heart, the navel, the base of the spine, and the opening of the sexual organ.

Running parallel to the central channel are the two other channels, the right channel (which is red in color) and the left channel (which is white in color). They connect to the central channel at the navel center and end at the nostrils. The right and left channels wrap around the central channel at the chakras, constricting it in such a way that the subtle energies called winds are not able to flow freely through it. In order to achieve enlightenment, the winds must be able to flow freely through the central channel, and much tantric practice is devoted to making this possible. It is essential to loosen the knots in the central channel because of what resides there.

For located in the center of the chakra at the heart is something called the "indestructible drop," the size of a tiny pea, white on the top and red on the bottom. Locked inside this drop is what is called the "mind of clear light," the most subtle form of consciousness. In order to achieve Buddhahood, the mind of clear light must be unlocked and allowed to "dawn." This is why the knots in the central channel must be loosened.

It is the mind of clear light, the most profound and fundamental form of consciousness, that travels from lifetime to lifetime. It is present at the moment of conception, where it becomes encased in the indestructible drop, formed from the red blood (the ovum) of the mother and the white semen (the sperm) of the father. Unless it is released through tantric practice, it will remain there until death, when, through a series of dissolutions, the winds that are the mounts of consciousness withdraw from our extremities and from our senses, to gather above and below the heart chakra. The mind of clear light is released at that moment, dawning for an instant before it goes on to the next lifetime, the next body. This dawning is a moment so brief that, in the trauma of death, it easily goes unnoticed.

However, we receive glimpses of the mind of clear light before death during the course of our lives—when we fall asleep, when we wake up, when we faint, when we go into a dream, when we come out of a dream, and, importantly, during orgasm. It is for this reason that we find in tantric Buddhism various forms of dream yoga and sexual yoga, with "yoga" meaning not the postures done in yoga class but profound forms of meditation. One such form of meditation, central to many tantric systems in Buddhism, might be called "psychic heat."

One of the hallmarks of tantric practice is visualization; another is the central importance of sacred syllables called *mantras*. In this practice, one visualizes the central channel as a hollow tube running from the crown of the head to the base of the spine. One then focuses the mind on the chakra located in the belly, said to be four finger breadths below the navel. In a number of tantric systems, one is supposed to visualize a vertical ink stroke, wider at the top and narrower at the bottom, inside the central channel. As one focuses one's mind on it, one imagines that it begins to become hot, glowing red. Flames begin to rise up through the central channel, causing a white drop of energy to descend down the central channel. As it passes through each of the chakras, one experiences different feelings of bliss.

Finally, it reaches the tip of the sexual organ. However, instead of the experience of the emission of orgasm, the feeling of bliss reverses course, moving upward through the central channel, again causing profound feelings of bliss as it travels upward to the crown of the head. Through this process, it is said that the mind of clear light will dawn. When properly recognized, through bringing about the union of bliss and emptiness, Buddhahood is achieved.

All of this is very complicated; this is a simplified description. It is considered one of the most advanced practices in all of Buddhism, requiring deep levels of concentration and particular powers of visualization. It is not something intended for the casual meditator. The Buddha created the game of baseball as a way to offer a tantric meditation that is accessible to everyone, players and fans alike.

In keeping with the idea that in tantra the extraordinary is to be found in the ordinary, the Buddha provides the secret teaching as an improbable response to what seems a most mundane question. A woman rises from her seat in the stands and politely asks the Buddha why baseball is so boring. It turns that she is not alone. The players themselves—on the field, in the dugout, in the bullpen—complain to the Buddha about their boredom.

The Buddha's answer is initially brief. He begins by saying that he made baseball boring because life is boring, and he created the game of baseball to teach players and fans about life, as he clearly has done in the preceding chapters of *The Baseball Sutra*. But then he says that he has made baseball boring so that players and fans can "practice the secret teaching that bestows great bliss." At that, Ted Williams, recently revealed to be the human incarnation of Vajrapani, the wrathful bodhisattva of power, asks the Buddha, as only Ted Williams would, to reveal "the goddamn secret teaching."

The Buddha describes a meditation practice. We tend to think of meditation as requiring a particular posture, specifically the lotus posture, in which the left foot is placed on the right thigh and the right foot is placed on the left thigh. However, unless one has taken many yoga classes, this posture can be painful. Here, the Buddha explains that this is a meditation practice that one can do sitting in the stands, in the dugout, in the bullpen, or sitting at home in front of the television. One simply needs to sit upright, with the spine straight and the shoulders level. In most meditation practice in Buddhism, one places the hands in what is called the position of equipoise, with the right palm resting on the left palm and the thumbs touching above, forming a circle.

In *The Baseball Sutra*, the Buddha teaches a new position similar to this classic pose, with a baseball held in that circle. Before providing the secret teaching, the Buddha instructs us to begin with a preliminary practice to calm and focus the mind, what might be called "baseball mindfulness," holding the ball in our lap and watching the action, absorbing ourselves in each pitch, each play, each decision made by each player as the ball moves around the diamond.

The Buddha then sets forth the secret teaching. He

describes the central channel that runs from the base
of the spine to the crown of the head. Immediately, the
baseball imagery is clear. The right and left channel that
weave around the central channel are red and white, the
colors of a baseball, intertwined like the stitches of a baseball. At the center of the chest is a tiny baseball, or the
"indestructible drop" as it is called in tantra, the size of
a tiny pea; "pea," of course, is slang for a fastball. The
Buddha notes that the tiny ball has 108 stitches, which a
baseball also has. He does not mention the significance of
this, because it would be known to any Buddhist—108 is
a sacred number in Buddhism. For example, in Tibetan
Buddhism there are 108 volumes in the canon of sacred
scriptures and 108 beads on a rosary. In Japan, the bells of
Buddhist temples are rung 108 times at midnight of the
New Year to dispel the 108 afflictions.

Just as the Buddha reveals that the true translation of
"Vajrapani" is "batter," we see that the tiny vertical ink
stroke that stands upright in the middle of the central
channel below the navel, wider at the top and narrower
at the bottom, is in reality a tiny baseball bat, ready to
hit the tiny baseball. Here, devotees of baseball, whether
players or fans, practice their own form of visualization.
Rather than imagining themselves to be a peaceful or
wrathful deity, they are to imagine themselves as the
bodhisattva of power, Vajrapani, but in the form of their
favorite player.

It is the bottom of the ninth of Game Seven of the World Series. Your team is down by a run. There are two outs and a runner on second. You, the batter, are extremely tiny, stepping into a tiny batter's box next to a tiny home plate. You focus on this visualization until it becomes sharp and clear, then visualize taking some practice swings and pointing the bat out toward the center field stands, like Ruth calling his shot at Wrigley Field in Game Three of the 1932 World Series. As you hold the bat, it begins to feel warm in your hands. All of this is occurring as one sits in meditation, so that everything is facing upward. The tiny batter points his tiny bat toward the top of the meditator's head.

You, the meditator, still visualized as your favorite professional hitter, imagine the tiny red and white pea, the indestructible drop, a baseball coming toward you right down the pike, down the central channel, toward the heart of the plate. It is a hundred-mile-per-hour fastball, but as great hitters have said over the years, when you're on a hot streak and seeing the ball well, the game slows down. You therefore see the ball coming toward you in slow motion. Deciding to swing, you remember everything you learned in the chapter called "Hips: Where the Action Is" in Ted Williams' book *The Science of Hitting*. You cock your hips, begin your stride, and start your swing. You strike the ball perfectly, smelling smoke when the horsehide hits the wood.

Although the ball is hit with record-setting exit velocity, everything again happens in slow motion. As the ball ascends through the central channel to the heart chakra, visualized as the pitcher's mound, the batter and the fans, hearing that distinctive crack of the bat of a well-struck ball, feel the bliss of anticipation that it might go out. As the ball ascends through the central channel to the throat chakra, visualized as center field, the center fielder, playing shallow so that he can throw out the runner at the plate if the hit is a single, stands frozen at his position, not even bothering to run to the warning track. Seeing this, the batter and the fans feel the bliss of confidence. As the ball ascends to the chakra at the crown of the head, going beyond the wall of Yankee Stadium, the batter and the fans feel the bliss of ecstasy. The ball is caught by a little girl who brought her glove to the game. The bliss of the child exceeds all others, and this bliss, as if by magic, pervades the bodies and minds of all beings.

This secret teaching is something that all players and fans, including pitchers, can practice, wherever they may be. Despite its deep tantric profundity, it is simple, requiring only five minutes and a love of the game.

9

ENLIGHTENMENT

Then Jackie Robinson emerged from the visitors' dug-out, wearing not Dodger Blue but the red and white of the Kansas City Monarchs. He came to the plate and said this to the Buddha: "World-Honored One, I was also Vajrapani, appearing first in the Negro Leagues, then on the Montreal Royals, and then on the Dodgers. In my first season in the majors, I was Vajrapani in his peaceful form, practicing the perfection of patience. In my second season, I was Vajrapani in his wrathful form, stealing second with spikes flashing. I have practiced the secret teaching for many seasons, allowing me to be an All-Star for six consecutive years, although I was already twenty-eight when I played my first major league game. Yet this secret teaching that you have revealed is a practice of heroics and home runs. In *The Baseball Sutra*, you have taught us about the impermanence of baseball, the sufferings of baseball, the emptiness of baseball. Tell us now, players and fans alike, how this wondrous game you have created teaches us how to live our lives."

The Buddha replied, "You speak the truth, you of the retired number on every team. Many thousands of players have played in the major leagues, many thousands more in the Negro Leagues and women's leagues. Then there are the minor leagues, the Little Leagues, and the softball leagues, fast pitch and slow. And this is only in this Northern Continent. In the Southern Continent and in the Eastern Continent there are so many more. Many millions around the world and across the centuries have played this game called baseball. Still, only some two hundred have achieved nirvana and entered the shrine at Cooperstown.

"Even in the major leagues, baseball is the game of the bullpen catchers, the utility infielders, the fourth outfielders, the mop-up pitchers, the journeymen, the farmhands, the September call-ups. It is the game for the casual fan and the die-hard fan. It is the game for those who suffer. I teach *The Baseball Sutra* for all players and all fans, so that they can understand the impermanence of baseball, the suffering of baseball, the emptiness of baseball, so that they can know these things and yet watch the game with contentment, that they may root for the home team, with the knowledge that if they don't win, it's a shame. So that they can take the lessons of this game into their life both on and off the field, engaging in all their deeds with insight, compassion, and non-attachment, not to retreat into the clubhouse to play poker but to take their position on the field, with their teammates, to play the game knowing full well that it will always end in loss. I teach players and fans alike to turn the game into the path.

"Wherever a father or mother plays catch with a son of good lineage or a daughter of good lineage, that place becomes a pure land. And if at the time of their death that son of good lineage or daughter of good lineage thinks of the mountain and the diamond, I will appear at their deathbed and deliver them to the diamond that is eternal, surviving the destruction that comes at the end of this degenerate age." Thus spoke the Buddha.

Rising to their feet, the managers, the coaches, the trainers, the broadcasters, the writers, the general managers, the hot dog vendors, the peanut vendors, the grounds crew, stadium security, and all the players and fans stood and cheered the words of the Buddha. So ends *The Baseball Sutra*.

Commentary

The visualization of the batted ball rising through the central channel to the crown of the head is an advanced tantric practice. But there is another form of tantric practice that is very different, a practice in which the ultimate is found in the ordinary. This is a practice associated with a group of Buddhist teachers in ancient India called the *mahāsiddhas*, which is translated literally as the "great accomplished ones" but which might also be translated as the "great magicians." Their greatest feat was to achieve enlightenment without becoming monks or nuns, finding enlightenment in the everyday.

Traditionally, there were eighty-four of these great magicians, more than enough to field two teams when the rosters used to expand to forty on August 31. Some were monks and some were kings, but most were ordinary men and women from the working classes: potters, tailors, farmers, blacksmiths, bakers, cobblers, weavers. In their stories, they typically are approached by a monk who asks for food. Although they themselves are poor, they share their food with the monk. In return, the monk provides them with a tantric teaching that they can practice while they work, in the midst of their daily labors. For example, a monk taught the cobbler to use the awl of his teachings to drill through the leather of his misconceptions to make the shoe of enlightenment. The blacksmith was told to think of himself as the blacksmith of consciousness, beating the iron of desire, anger, and ignorance in the fire of knowledge. The message of all the stories is that the most profound reality is to be found in the most mundane tasks, that enlightenment is present in each of the thoughts we have throughout the day. We just have to see it.

The Buddha created the game of baseball in order to

provide the opportunity for this insight. For the player and the coach, what is more ordinary, and monotonous, than throwing and catching the ball, taking infield practice, shagging flies, doing sliding drills, taking batting practice. For the fan, what is more ordinary, and monotonous, than the slow pace of the game, the litany of foul pops into the stands, strikeouts, walks, weakly hit grounders to short, lazy fly balls. And this is not to mention all the sitting around—the players in the dugout waiting for their turn to bat, the fans in the stands sitting through pitching changes and between-inning breaks. Indeed, for the player and the fan, everything about baseball is ordinary, everything about baseball is familiar. This is what makes it the perfect game, both for understanding suffering and for understanding how to transcend suffering.

Tantric practice is often compared to alchemy, the transmutation of base metals into gold. In tantra, it is the transmutation of the negative emotions, what Buddhism calls the poisons, into the cure for the poisons. In this game created by the Buddha, it is baseball that is transmuted, into a state of mind that does not renounce the poisons, a state of mind that imbibes the poisons in order to transcend them. Baseball is a place where the poisons of desire, anger, and ignorance are indulged, where desire, anger, and ignorance are necessary, where desire, anger, and ignorance are encouraged.

Desire drives so much of the game for player and fan. For the player and fan focused on the game, whether their team is at bat or in the field, every pitch is an occasion for desire. For the batter, it is desire to get the hit, the big hit, the clutch hit, the walk-off. Or at least to work a walk, put down a bunt, hit a fly ball deep enough to score the runner from third, go the other way to move the runner over. For the pitcher it is desire for the out— even better, the strikeout, and even better the swinging strikeout, the batter unable to catch up with the fastball, the batter swinging over the sinker. For the fielder, it is the desire to make the play—even better, the leaping catch, the diving catch, the circus catch, the jump throw from short, the throw from the knees from third, the game-saving play. The fan wants all these things as well. And together, player and fan want the win.

Anger is also essential to the game. For the player it is above all anger at oneself for not doing those things one desires. For the batter, the fielder, the pitcher, the catcher, and the fan, there is anger at the home plate umpire for missing a call, for having a strike zone that is at once too big for the hitter and too small for the pitcher. For the fan, there is anger at the other team for robbing the batter of a hit, or at the player for making an error, for making a bonehead play, for missing the cutoff man, for running through the stop sign. There is anger at the fan who prevents the first baseman from reaching into the stands to catch a pop-up. And, of course, there is anger at losing.

And finally, there is ignorance. Again, in Buddhism, ignorance is not a lack of some knowledge—of the knowledge of the rules of the game, the knowledge of baseball history, the knowledge of who had the most steroid-free home runs in his career, the knowledge of advanced analytics. Ignorance is a misunderstanding of the nature of reality. Ignorance is the belief in self. In baseball, ignorance is the belief in the illusion of the team. It is the belief that there is something called the Yankees that moves up and down in the standings, that exists from season to season, that exists from game to game. That this thing called the Yankees is a place for our hopes and dreams, something that can lift us to the heights of ecstasy and plunge us into the depths of despair. That this thing called the Yankees is something we can love, and that therefore gives us something we can hate (the Red Sox).

When Buddhists describe the immediate causes of suffering, the actions motivated by desire, anger, and ignorance that create negative karma and thus suffering in the future, they list ten sins, or "non-virtues": killing, stealing, sexual misconduct, deceit, divisive speech, harsh speech, senseless speech, coveting, wishing harm, and wrong view. Yet nine of these ten sins occur on the field of play in each game and have no negative consequence whatsoever. In each game there are twin killings, stealing of bases, stealing of signs, robbing of homers, the deceit of the changeup, the divisive speech of chatter, the harsh speech directed at the home plate umpire, the coveting of wins, saves, and rings, the wish for the other team to boot the ball, and the wrong view that any of this ultimately matters.

The Buddha created the game of baseball as a place where we can drink the three poisons of desire, anger, and ignorance—from the water cooler in the dugout, from the plastic cups passed down the row to us from the vendor—and not suffer serious consequences. There's no dying in baseball. The Buddha created the game of baseball as a place where desire, anger, and ignorance are essential, but where their fallacy is forever on the field. We cannot play the game, we cannot watch the game without the desire to win, without the expectation of victory, without rooting for the home team. We cannot play the game, we cannot watch the game without hating to lose, without hating the umpire. And we cannot play the game, we cannot watch the game without the ignorance that believes in a team. In *The Baseball Sutra*, the Buddha teaches us why each of these desires, each of these hatreds, rests on fundamental forms of ignorance.

In *The Baseball Sutra*, the players and fans assembled around the Buddha at Yankee Stadium learn the truth of suffering. They recount in painful detail all the forms of suffering, great and small, that suffuse the game. The Buddha explains that these sufferings teach us, as no other game can, the suffering of pain, the suffering of change, and the suffering of conditioning. Because suffering occurs with each pitch of each game, baseball teaches us that the desire for lasting happiness is futile. It is not to be found on the diamond.

In *The Baseball Sutra*, the players and fans assembled around the Buddha at Yankee Stadium learn the truth of impermanence. They recount in painful detail how things fall apart so quickly and unexpectedly, over the course of a game, over the course of a season, over the course of a career. With everything in a state of flux, with disaster able to strike in the next moment, baseball teaches us that hatred only causes us pain, that there is nothing worth hating. The Buddha created a game in which there is a pitch called the circle change.

In *The Baseball Sutra*, the players and fans assembled around the Buddha at Yankee Stadium learn from the Buddha the most fundamental truth, the truth of no self. It is this truth that makes desire and hatred not something we have to suppress, but that makes them impossible. This is the truth of emptiness, where the team—the place in which we invest such great hopes, the thing that soothes us with desire and protects us with hatred—is an illusion. It never existed, it does not exist, it never will exist. The Buddha created a game of endless changes, of substitutions, double switches, roster moves, call-ups, sent-downs, and injured lists to confront us each day with the startling fact that there are no Yankees.

And yet the fact that baseball is emptiness and emptiness is baseball does not mean that we should not play the game; it does not mean that we should not watch the game; it does not mean that we should not pull for the Yankees. The Buddha created the game of baseball so that we can see a mirage, know it to be an illusion, and yet bask in its beauty. The Buddha created the game of baseball so that we could indulge our desire, our hatred, and our ignorance without being harmed by them, as we are harmed by them outside the stadium. In the safe space of the friendly confines, we are not harmed by desire, hatred, and ignorance, because the Buddha has taught us to see their true nature. We aspire to become one day like the enlightened masters, like Stengel, La Russa, and Torre, with no particular investment in the outcome, no allegiance to the team, no identification with the club, but simply the playing out of the endless possibilities of the endless game, where anything can happen and everything can happen, the eternal unfolding. As the Buddha says, "I teach players and fans alike to turn the game into the path."

The Buddha's final statement in a sutra is considered particularly important, and so we should repeat his final statement in *The Baseball Sutra*. He says, "Wherever a father or mother plays catch with a son of good lineage or a daughter of good lineage, that place becomes a pure land. And if at the time of their death that son of good lineage or daughter of good lineage thinks of the mountain and the diamond, I will appear at their deathbed and deliver them to the diamond that is eternal, surviving the destruction that comes at the end of this degenerate age."

In Buddhism, "son of good lineage" and "daughter of good lineage" do not mean someone from an aristocratic background or a wealthy family. They mean someone who has compassion for others. The Buddha says that we do not need to go to the trouble of buying an expensive ticket, fighting traffic, paying for parking, walking to the gates, and going through security in order for the benefits of baseball to be bestowed upon us. We simply need to play catch. All that is needed is two gloves, one ball, a setting sun, and some open space away from windows.

All the truths of baseball can be found in this most precious of childhood pastimes, where the lessons of the game are passed from parent to child—how to get down for a grounder, how to get under a fly, how to catch the ball with two hands, how to watch the ball into the mitt—where the child can dispel their inevitable frustrations toward the parent by throwing a ball at the parent's head as hard as they can, without fear of punishment, and with the parent offering instruction in how to throw it harder and more accurately toward the cranial target. So much of the complicated relationship of parent and child is played out by playing catch. And we must recall that in Buddhism, because of the endless cycle of rebirth, each being has been our parent in a past life, so that whenever we play catch with anyone, we are playing catch with our parent.

The Buddha says that wherever we play this most perfect game, that place will be transformed into a pure land, a place of peace and happiness, protected from the three types of suffering. And he says that when our parents are gone and we lie on our own deathbed, the Buddha who created this game of baseball for us will appear at our bedside in the guise of the third-base coach of our favorite team, his right arm twirling, waving us home.

APPENDIX

The Baseball Sutra

1

THE PROLOGUE

Thus did I hear. At one time, the Buddha was residing in the pure land called Yankee Stadium in the city of New York in the land of America in the Western Continent. As he stood near the center of the green mandala, a great rumbling was heard. Beneath his flat feet, each marked with the image of a ball, a great mountain rose from the earth, a full fourteen finger breadths in height. Around that mountain, a smaller mandala in the shape of a diamond magically appeared, with a border of sand from the River Ganges, a cushion of the finest Benares silk at three corners. Atop the great mountain there was a slab of alabaster, pure white in color, two cubits long and eight finger breadths wide. Here the Buddha stood.

The mountain was surrounded by a great assembly of immortals, gods, and demigods of the past and the present, each gathered at his position in the ten directions of the pure land. At the first square in the east stood Gehrig, Moose, Pepitone, Mattingly, and Martinez. At the second square in the north stood Richardson,

Randolph, Soriano, and Canó. At the third square in the west stood McDougald, Boyer, Nettles, and Brosius. At the place between the second square and the third square stood Rizzuto, Kubek, and Jeter. At the place called the household in the south crouched Berra, Howard, Munson, and Posada, each adorned with the tools of ignorance, each flashing signs. In the place called the right in the northeast stood Ruth, Maris, Jackson, Sweet Lou, O'Neill, Godzilla, and Judge. In the place called the center in the north stood DiMaggio, Mantle, Murcer, and Bernie. In the place called the left in the northwest stood White, Winfield, and Gardner. Standing at the foot of the mountain, surrounding the Buddha, stood Ford, Reynolds, Gomez, Terry, Stottlemyre, Gator, Catfish, Key, Pettitte, Cone, Boomer, El Duque, Moose, Sabathia, and Mo. To the Buddha's left side in a narrow cave dug out of the earth sat Stengel, Houk, Showalter, and Torre.

Beyond the field sat row upon row of laymen and laywomen, reaching almost to the heavens. In the row nearest to the field sat the laymen named Rickey and Miller. High above in a box sat the preachers Barber, Allen, McCarver, Singleton, Kay, Sterling, and Waldman, the scribes Angell, Verducci, Madden, Olney, Kepner, and Sherman. In another box sat men called Stick and Cash. Seated alone high above was the one of gentle voice and perfect pronunciation of all names in all languages, called the Herder of Sheep.

At that time, without speaking, the Buddha performed a mudra that united the opposites. He did not need a glove; all buddhas have webbed fingers. His right hand made the gesture of the circle change. The index finger of his left hand pointed down, calling for a fastball, then two fingers pointing down for a curveball, then three fingers pointing down for a slider. And then, he emitted a ray of light from between his eyebrows that illuminated all ten directions from the three divisions of east, central, and west of the American and the National, from the highest heavens of the major leagues to the deepest hells of Low A.

All the gods in the pure land and the laypeople in the stands were perplexed by this sight. The bodhisattva called The Baby said to the bodhisattva called The Horse of Iron, "I have long dwelled in this pure land, yet never have I seen the Buddha perform such a miracle. I ask you to explain it to me, you who followed me in the line and who brought me home so many times." The Horse of Iron replied, "It was a long ago, in another pure land called the Old Yankee Stadium where it was only 295 down the right field line. You were there that day but you do not remember, for between innings you had eaten many hot dogs. On that day, the Buddha also emitted a ray of light from between his eyebrows, illuminating all the leagues in the ten directions. Then he preached what is called *The Baseball Sutra*. I believe he will now preach that *Baseball Sutra* again."

Then the bodhisattva known as Seven stood, put on his batting helmet, and addressed the Buddha: "Lord, in the past when you set forth *The Baseball Sutra*, the gods of this pure land named Yankee Stadium lived their whole lives in this abode, unless they were banished to Kansas City. At that time, as the Buddha of our pure land, you taught this precious sutra only to us. Having meditated on your teaching in the clubhouse, during batting practice, in the on-deck circle, during rainouts, and in the dugout, we your devoted disciples went from victory to victory, defeating our enemies in four, five, six, or seven games. Today, because of free agency, our enemies become our friends, our friends become our enemies. Thus, I beseech you to teach *The Baseball Sutra* to all the gods of all the pure lands."

The Buddha smiled upon the Commerce Comet, saying, "Well done, well done, child of good slugging percentage, wearer of the Triple Crown. You speak the truth. In the world of baseball on this day, among the gods, there is no friend or enemy. It is only the multitudes who abide in the bleachers who bear enmity throughout their lifetimes. Therefore, I shall teach *The Baseball Sutra* to all the gods."

The laymen and laywomen seated on the borders of the mandala began to boo, each in their own language, silenced only when The Baby stood to speak. Adjusting his jockstrap, he addressed the Buddha. "Lord, I do not understand. Your pure land is full, its field filled with Yankees, its seats filled with fans. Our abbots sit in the dugout. The only empty space is the dugout of our enemies, who abide there only for three days or four days, or one day to make up a rainout. Yet the gods of the other pure lands are many. There is no space to fit the gods of the Eastern Division of the American League, much less the gods of all the divisions of all the leagues."

The Buddha replied, "Did you come for the dharma or did you come for the dugout? Bambino, you should know that the powers of the Buddha are inconceivable, able to fill the visitors' dugout with all of the gods of the other pure lands, without changing the size of the gods and without changing the size of the dugout." The Buddha again emitted rays of light from the space between his eyes, the color of a blue pinstripe. Yet, as if by a miracle, as those rays approached the other pure lands, they turned into the color of that pure land—blue for the pure land of the Dodgers, red for the pure land of the Cardinals, green for the pure land of the A's, orange for the pure land of the Mets.

As they reached those pure lands, the rays of light were transformed into all manner of gifts for the gods:

gloves, bats, cleats, batting helmets, batting gloves, elbow protectors, catcher's masks, car dealerships, deodorant commercials, and postgame radio shows. Delighted, the gods of the other pure lands boarded their team planes and flew to the city of New York, landing there in the time it takes for a man to bend his arm. After an hour spent in traffic, they arrived at the pure land called Yankee Stadium.

First to enter the stadium were the gods from Boston, led by The Kid, a god who does not tip his cap. He was followed by gods named Yaz, Tiant, Evans, Lynn, Big Papi, and Pedro. From Baltimore came gods named Palmer, Boog, Murray, Cal, and two gods named Robinson. From Seattle came gods named the Big Unit, Junior, Edgar, and Ichiro. From Detroit came Kaline, Freehan, Lolich, Trammell, Whitaker, and Verlander. From San Francisco came Mays, Marichal, McCovey, Cepeda, Clark, and Posey. From Minnesota came Oliva, Killebrew, Kaat, Carew, and Mauer. From Philadelphia came gods named Lefty, Allen, Schmidt, Rollins, and Utley. From Milwaukee came gods named The Hammer, Mathews, Spahn, Yount, and Molitor. From the pure land of Montreal came gods named Vlad, Rock, The Hawk, and Carter. From Toronto came Alomar, Halladay, Delgado, and He of the Constant Helmet. From St. Louis, gods named The Man, Gibson, Boyer, Simmons, Pujols, Molina, and the Wizard of

Oz. From Cleveland, Colavito, Thome, and Omar. From Pittsburgh, Clemente, Stargell, Parker, and McCutchen. From Queens, gods named Seaver, Straw, Doc, Hernandez, and Wright. From one Los Angeles, Koufax, Drysdale, Fernando, Hershiser, Piazza, and Kershaw. From the other Los Angeles, Grich, Joyner, and the fish, Salmon and Trout. From Houston, Bagwell, Biggio, and Richard. From Oakland, Rickey, Rudi, and Blue. From one Chicago, Banks, Santo, Buckner, Sandberg, Jenkins, and Wood. From the other Chicago, gods named Minnie, Little Louie, Baines, and the Big Hurt. From Atlanta, gods named Murphy, Chipper, Smoltz, Glavine, Mad Dog, and Crime Dog. From Cincinnati, Pinson, Flood, Bench, and Morgan. From Texas, Von Ryan's Express and Pudge. From Kansas City, Brett, McRae, Saberhagen, and Bo. From San Diego, a god named Tony. From the old Washingtons, the Big Train, Hondo, Brinkman, and Osteen. From Tampa came Longoria, Price, and Crawford. From Miami came Sheffield, Cabrera, and Leiter. From Arizona, came Schilling, Grace, and Finley. From Colorado came Walker, Helton, and Bichette. And from an ancient league came gods named Satchel, Josh, Buck, and Cool Papa. Finally, summoned by the Buddha from the realm of the hungry ghosts, came a god with no shoes.

When all the gods had found their places in the dugout, the Buddha declared: "Now, I will set forth

The Baseball Sutra for the benefit of the many, for the happiness of the many, out of compassion for the world, for the welfare, the benefit, and the happiness of players and fans." Yet before he could begin, five hundred gods stood up and made their way across the field toward the bullpen exit. Among them were gods named Rocket, Barry, Big Mac, Sammy, A-Rod, Manny, Rafael, Miguel, Vaughn, Brown, Braun, and the King of Hits. Others rose to stop them, but the Buddha said, "Let them go. It will be many eons before they enter nirvana." Thus spoke the Buddha.

2

THE QUESTION

Then, by the power of the Buddha, the yogi named Berra stood, lifted his mask, and addressed the Buddha. "Lord, as you stood atop the mountain forty cubits from where I squat, you showed first one finger, then two fingers, then three. He who catches the ball must make these signs from behind the white platter. Yet the Blessed One made them toeing the slab atop the mountain. I am confused. Please explain the meaning of these three signs."

The Buddha replied, "Well said, well said, notorious bad-ball hitter, three-time MVP. What you say is true. Now, listen to my words: When I made three signs from atop the mountain, their meaning was not fastball, curveball, and slider. They had a hidden meaning, a meaning that I reveal to you this day. Just as there are three strikes, so there are three signs that mark everything in the lives of players and fans. What are those three? They are impermanence, suffering, and no self. I teach these three signs so that all beings may be liberated from sorrow and find the peace of nirvana.

"Yet these three signs are difficult to understand for those of low OPS. And so I have created this game called baseball, played in the diamond realm, so that gods and humans might understand and find peace. It is the game of odd numbers: three outs, three strikes, nine innings, twenty-seven outs. It is the best of games, superior to the games of the unenlightened, for it teaches that the cycle of birth and death is endless, extending to infinity. Like the cycle of birth itself, the game can last forever. The games of the unenlightened have quarters and halves, shot clocks and two-minute warnings. In baseball, there can be extra innings extending over innumerable eons. The highest possible ERA for the caster of ball is infinity. And why? If he is lifted in his first start with even one run scored without an out being recorded, the ERA is infinity. The number of strikeouts possible in a single inning is infinity. And why? If the batter reaches base on a wild pitch or passed ball on the third strike, the maximum number of strikeouts is infinity. The number of pitches a batter can foul off with two outs and two strikes in the bottom of the ninth is infinity. The number of innings that the teams can play is infinity.

"Yet just as a plantain tree grows, abides, decays, and dies, so does each game have its phases of early innings, middle innings, late innings, and the final out. Dying and reborn, the teams play again the next day (unless it rains), 162 times, as many as 182 if there is a tiebreaker and they go to what is renowned as the seventh game. And then there's always next year." Thus spoke the Buddha.

3

IMPERMANENCE

Then John "Mayor" Lindsey, wearing the uniform of the New Jersey Jackals, rose and addressed the Blessed One. "Lord, I was drafted in the thirteenth round by the Rockies and played A Ball for seven years for the Portland Rockies, the Asheville Tourists, and the Salem Red Sox. Then I was signed by the Mariners and played A Ball for the San Bernardino Stampede before ascending to Double-A, where I played for the San Antonio Missions. Then I descended to the Single-A Jupiter Hammerheads and then to the independent league New Jersey Jackals. Then I signed with the Dodgers and played for the Triple-A Las Vegas 51s and then their Double-A affiliate, the Jacksonville Suns. Lord, you may know them as the Jacksonville Jumbo Shrimp. Then I signed with the Marlins and played for their Double-A New Orleans Zephyrs. Lord, you may know them as the New Orleans Baby Cakes. Then I signed with the Dodgers again and played for the Triple-A Albuquerque Isotopes of the Pacific Coast League. Lord, after sixteen years in the minors, I was called up by the Dodgers. I wore Dodger Blue for eleven games. I had one hit in twelve at bats before I was hit by a pitch and broke my hand. Later, I was signed by the Tigers and played for the Toledo Mud Hens. And then I was released.

"Blessed One, counting the Mexican League and winter ball I played 2,277 games in the minors for twenty-five teams over twenty-one years. I drove for endless miles in old buses with bad air-conditioning. I ate countless bad meals of fried food with plastic forks. I loaded countless suitcases on and off buses. I slept in countless bad hotels with stained carpets, coin-operated Magic Fingers beds, and no Wi-Fi. I sat for countless hours on hard benches in concrete dugouts. I took countless showers in cinder-block clubhouses. I played on countless bad fields and played countless bad hops before tiny crowds. And yet my lifetime average in the majors was only .083.

"O Teacher of Players and Fans, taking off my first baseman's mitt, I ask: Why did you make a game so filled with change?"

"O son of the A leagues, I made this game to teach the truth of impermanence, that all things are subject to change, that all things will one day fall apart. I teach that the hot streak leads to the slump, that .300 leads to the Mendoza Line, that the hundred-mile-per-hour heater leads to Tommy John surgery, that the perfect game through six leads to the loss after nine, that the big league contract leads to being designated for assignment.

"I teach the wandering between worlds, where the players in the heavens called the majors are blown by the winds of their statistics to the hells of the minors. I teach that the denizens of Triple A toil in game after game, meeting a god only when that god descends for a rehab assignment and pays for the spread. I teach that even for those who ascend, the time is short, able to wear the garments of the gods only in spring training before being returned to hell, the domain of demeaning team logos.

"I made this game not to make players suffer but to make players see that to be attached to luxury suites, private jets, and Gatorade commercials is only a source of suffering. I made this game to teach players to play without attachment." Thus spoke the Buddha.

4

SUFFERING

In the broadcast booth, Kitty took off his headset, rose from his seat next to Bob Costas, and addressed the Buddha. "Lord, in my twenty-five years in the majors, I have toed the slab many times. I started 625 games, I won 283 games, I pitched 180 complete games. In those games, I saw so much suffering. I saw pitchers get hammered, throw wild pitches, not have their good stuff, hang curveballs, leave sinkers up in the zone, miss the corners, be wild in the strike zone. I saw infielders have easy grounders go through the wickets, I saw them come off the bag, miss tags, throw wide of the bag, be handcuffed by a bad hop, and olé ground balls down the line. I saw outfielders misplay flies for triples, mistime their jump, trap sinking liners, have fly balls bounce off the heel of their glove, miss the cutoff man, airmail throws to third, and short-hop throws to the plate. I saw catchers get hit by foul tips, drop pop-ups, miss tags, drop throws, commit passed balls, and get crossed up. I saw runners get picked off first, overslide the bag at second, make the first out of the inning at third, and run through the stop sign to be out by a mile at home. I saw batters bunt foul with two strikes, miss a sign, hit a line drive into the shift, take a called third strike with men on base after being ahead in the count 3-0, swing at balls that bounce in front of the plate.

"Blessed One, you have made a game where the best batters fail to get a hit 70 percent of the time, where the scoreboard in every stadium each day displays a giant E, where a 'quality start' yields a 4.50 ERA, where relief pitchers are judged not by their wins but by their saves, the number of times they avert disaster. A team that loses four of every ten games always goes to the playoffs; a team that loses five of every ten games never does. All of this takes place in a season that seems endless, 162 games, many endured in the dog days of August. Blessed One, holding high one of my sixteen Gold Gloves, I ask you: Why did you make a game so suffused with suffering?"

The Buddha responded, "Well said, well said, Original Twin, you, who should be in the Hall of Fame. You speak the truth. I have made a game in which there are so many ways to fail, and those failures are recorded for all time, for all to see, and for all to ponder. I made this game to teach the truth of suffering.

"I teach the suffering of pain. This is the suffering known to all, the decline in a player's skills over the course of his career: the drop in bat speed for the hitter, the reduction in range for the fielder, the loss of miles per hour off the fastball for the pitcher. This is the suffering felt by each fan with each loss, felt by player and fan alike when the team does not make the playoffs. This is the suffering of player and fan alike in this game where most players have a good year among many bad years, not a bad year among many good years.

"I teach the suffering of change. This is when that which once seemed to be a source of pleasure becomes a source of pain. This is why I made a game that is long and can always be longer, where the excitement felt by fans upon entering the stadium and seeing the field of green as they make their way through the concourse turns into restlessness as the game moves into the late innings of a laugher. This is why I made a season that is so long, where the excitement of the players on Opening Day has been sapped by the trade deadline.

"I teach the suffering of conditioning, that each player on each team and each fan in each seat, and each fan watching at home and each fan listening in the car, is ready to undergo suffering in each moment. I have made a game where some three hundred pitches are thrown in each game and each of those pitches is a moment of failure for the pitcher or the hitter, for the fielder or the runner, and always for the fan of one team or the other. In order to teach the suffering of conditioning, I have made a game in which there are so many ways to fail." Thus spoke the Buddha.

5

NO SELF

Then, by the power of the Buddha, an old man rose from the upper deck along the third-base line. He wore a Yankees cap and a pinstripe jersey with the number 4. Removing his cap, he addressed the Buddha. "O, One Who Has Gone to Happiness, I have been a Yankees fan my whole life, from the time I watched the '27 Yankees as a seven-year-old boy in the old Yankee Stadium to the Yankees of today. Over the course of my life, the Yankees have been good and bad, they have won and lost. Thousands of players have worn the pinstripes, some remembered, most forgotten. Now, I am one hundred years old. When I watch a game from the stands, or on television, or listen to the radio, I sometimes ask myself, What are the Yankees? Where are the Yankees? These seem odd questions, easy to answer, and yet I am plagued with doubt. I ask the Enlightened One to enlighten me."

The Buddha replied, "You ask a wise question, O Season-Ticket Holder. I will answer your question with a question of my own. Imagine a Yankees roster on Opening Day, made up of eight position players, a backup catcher, a fourth outfielder, two utility infielders, a DH, five starters, five long relievers, a seventh-inning guy, an eighth-inning guy, and a closer. Imagine that because of pulled hamstrings, pulled groins, pulled lats, oblique strains, torn anterior cruciate ligaments, concussions from running into walls, hip pointers, hit batsmen, torn ulnar collateral ligaments, bone spurs, sore shoulders, bad knees, numb fingers, hangnails, slumps, errors, losing streaks, drug suspensions, high ERA, and low OBP, every member of the twenty-six-man Opening Day roster is placed on the injured list, sent down, traded, designated for assignment, or given his release at some point during the season. Imagine that on August 31, the day before the roster expands, not a single player from the Opening Day roster remains. My question to you, Old Man, is: Is this team on August 31 the Yankees? I answer your question by repeating your question back to you: Where are the Yankees?"

The old man said, "Lord, those Yankees are not the Yankees. They may wear the pinstripes, but they are not my team. I look for the Yankees among the players on the roster but I cannot find them." The Buddha declared, "Well said, you of many seventh-inning stretches. Let me now ask more questions, and answer them myself.

"Is Yankee Stadium the Yankees? No, for Yankee

Stadium was demolished and a new structure built on a new site. Is the franchise the Yankees? No, the franchise is something concocted by lawyers and bankers, to be bought and sold by those who may not have a single at bat. Is the logo the Yankees? No, because around the world, people wear the cap with the interlocking N and Y who do not know any of the retired numbers. Is it the memories of the fans? No, because the fans grow old and die, and their memories die with them. And so I declare, nowhere are the Yankees to be found. The Yankees do not exist. The Yankees are empty. The Yankees are not the Yankees. Therefore, they are the Yankees."

The World-Honored One continued: "You see that the householder wears the tools of ignorance, but all sentient beings, players and fans, wear the tools of ignorance each day. I made this game called baseball to teach fans, players, umpires, agents, scouts, front-office people, owners, league executives, vendors, ushers, groundskeepers, writers, and broadcasters that there is no team, there is no baseball. Baseball is emptiness. Emptiness is baseball. Baseball is not other than emptiness. Emptiness is not other than baseball.

"And why? The caster of the ball seeks the emptiness of the domain of the strike—whether inside or outside, high or low, above the knees, below the letters, on the black, catching the corner—the emptiness never tainted by wood, except for a caught foul tip. The fielder of the baseball seeks the empty space of his brother's glove, whether it be the guardian of the first square, the second square, the third square, or the guardian of the household, without short hops or airmail. The striker of the baseball seeks the empty space of the hole, the gap, down the line, the intermediate space between short and deep, the emptiness in the green grass at the foot of the mountain—to the left if the hurler falls off the mountain to the right, to the right if the hurler falls off the mountain to his left—and best of all the emptiness when the ball has gone, gone, gone beyond, gone completely beyond the wall. In emptiness, there are no Yankees."

Hearing these words, some players (from other teams) vomited blood, some players' heads split open, and fans killed themselves by jumping from the upper deck. The Buddha said, "These players and fans were not yet ready to hear the ultimate truth. But fear not—they will be reborn immediately in the pure land of Fenway Park." Thus spoke the Buddha.

6

KARMA

Then a New York City firefighter rose from the stands behind home plate, took off his helmet, and addressed the Buddha. "Blessed One, I have been a Yankees fan my entire life. I lost many brothers and sisters on September 11. That year, the Yankees won the pennant and faced the Diamondbacks in the World Series. They brought great hope to the city of New York in a time of grief. They had come-from-behind victories in Games Four and Five in extra innings, with dramatic home runs by Tino, Jeter, and Brosius. They went to Arizona for Game Seven, a tense pitching duel between Schilling and the Rocket, with Alfonso Soriano, he of the mammoth bat, hitting a solo shot in the eighth to put the Yankees up 2-1. Joe called in the greatest relief pitcher in history to close out the game and bring the trophy back to New York. And yet the Yankees lost. How is this possible?"

The Buddha said, "Nothing occurs by chance. Everything is the result of our past deeds. I will tell you a story. Long ago, there were three brothers, the sons of a merchant who served the king. One day, they climbed over the wall into the king's private gardens, where he had a menagerie of wild animals that he had tamed. The king's prized possession was a king cobra. The three boys were throwing a ball back and forth as they ran laughing through the garden. Suddenly, the middle brother threw the ball to the youngest brother. But the boy missed the ball. It struck the snake, killing it.

"The boys ran away in fear, but before they could climb back over the wall, they were captured by the king's soldiers, who took them before the king and told him what had happened. The king was enraged and had the brothers locked in the dungeon, declaring that the one who threw the ball and killed the snake would be executed the next day. The oldest brother stepped forth and declared that he had thrown the ball, even though he had not. The king proclaimed that he would be beheaded at dawn.

"That night, the three boys sat together in their cell, weeping at their fate. The royal jailer was a wise old man. He unlocked the door to the dungeon and came in. He told the boys that he had seen what happened, that the boys had not meant to kill the cobra, that it was the cobra's time to die, according to the law of karma. Unlocking the window of their cell, he told the boys to escape.

"The two younger brothers immediately jumped out

and ran home, but the oldest brother remained. He asked the old jailer, 'What will happen to you?' The jailer said that the next day, after the boys were safely home, he would go before the king, admit what he had done, and take his own life, standing at the foot of the throne. The boy refused to go, saying that he would not allow him to make such a sacrifice. But the jailer explained that he was an old man and had lived a good life. He was happy to give his life for an innocent child. The jailer again unlocked the window to the cell and held it open, telling the boy to go.

"In this lifetime, Scott Brosius was the older brother, Mariano Rivera was the middle brother, Derek Jeter was the youngest brother, and George Steinbrenner was the king. Because in a past life Mo had killed the serpent of the king, he suffered the consequences of his deed. Thus, when Damian Miller bunted to move the pinch runner over, Mo, instead of throwing a fastball to Jeter, threw a cutter that tailed away and into the outfield. Then, when Jay Bell laid down a sacrifice bunt to move the runner to third, Mo threw to Scott Brosius for the putout.

"Yet, Brosius did not throw to first for the double play, although Bell was old and a slow runner. Instead, he held the ball. And why? Because in that lifetime long ago, Jay Bell had been the old jailer of the king, who saved the lives of the three brothers. Scott Brosius does not remember his past lives. And yet, compelled by his past karma and the debt he owed to the old man, he held the ball. This in turn led to Gonzalez's broken-bat bloop over the drawn-in infield, allowing Jay Bell to score the winning run. And so the serpents won the series. Luis Gonzalez had been the snake. Scott Brosius bears no blame." Thus spoke the Buddha.

7

VAJRAPANI

Then Pudge Fisk, Son of the Sox, the red and the white, rose from his place at the household, adjusted his chest protector, and said, "Lord, long ago, in Fenway Park, the Splendid Splinter rode in a chariot to the middle of the mandala, surrounded by ninety-nine gods of the past century and all the All-Stars of the season. He turned to Big Mac and said, 'Son of St. Louis, when you foul one back, have you ever smelled smoke?' Lord, I was there that night and I heard those words, but I did not understand. What was the meaning of those words?"

The Buddha replied, "Son of the Sox, Teddy Ballgame spoke in the twi-night language, understood by only the initiates of the secret signs. He spoke of the esoteric teaching, revealed to few." He then was silent.

Soon the sound of a bat being taken from the bat rack was heard from the visitors' dugout. Ted Williams, tall and thin, The Kid of the 1941 season, as if cryogenically preserved, emerged from the dugout, walked to the on-deck circle, rubbed his bat with a bone, and knelt on one knee. The crowd roared, but Williams did not tip his cap. The Buddha then spoke, "O Last Man to Bat .400. Reveal your true nature."

At that time, The Thumper rose, holding his bat in his left hand. Suddenly he was enveloped by a blinding light, brighter than a billion night-game bulbs. From the light emerged a wrathful deity, dark blue in color, wreathed in flames, wearing a triple crown, a vajra held aloft in his left hand, striking fear into the hearts of the *Boston Globe* writers. The fans cringed in their seats; the players hid behind their gloves.

The Buddha said, "Fear not, children of good slugging percentage. Behold the bodhisattva Vajrapani. He has been worshiped for centuries across the continent of Asia, from the peaks of Tibet to the islands of Japan, as the bodhisattva of power—indeed, the embodiment of all the power of all the buddhas of the three times. He holds in his hand the vajra, this word difficult to understand by those of the Western continents, some calling it a diamond scepter, some calling it a thunderbolt.

"But these scholars of my teaching speak from ignorance. For if they were to see the most ancient rock carvings of my deeds—my birth, my enlightenment, my turning of the wheel of the dharma—they would see a mysterious figure to my left, holding a club in his left hand. This is the true Vajrapani. And today I reveal the true meaning of his name. 'Vajra' does not mean 'diamond scepter' or 'thunderbolt' or all the names one reads in books by those who call themselves scholars of Buddhism. The Sanskrit *vajra* means 'bat.' The Sanskrit word *pani* means 'hand.' 'Vajrapani' means 'one who holds the bat.' 'Vajrapani' means 'batter.'

"Some say that the game of baseball was invented by Abner Doubleday in America in 1839. This is the view of the benighted. Some say that the game of baseball was invented in England more than a century earlier. This is the view of the shortsighted. Archaeologists who excavate the ancient depictions of my deeds will see Vajrapani by my side, bat resting on his left shoulder, in carvings that are two thousand years old. I invented the game of baseball to teach the dharma, never teaching without my best batter by my side, just as the Old Professor never played a game without his man. All the buddhas of the past, all the buddhas of the present, and all the buddhas of the future create the game of baseball in age after age so that all beings, players and fans alike, can pass beyond sorrow.

"And in season after season, Vajrapani appears in uniform, bat in hand, from the Little Leagues, to Low A, to the majors, striking fear into the hearts of opposing pitchers. In the time of wars, Vajrapani appeared in the world as Ted Williams. And yet, over all these seasons, he has not revealed the secret teaching. There goes Vajrapani, the greatest hitter who ever lived." Thus spoke the Buddha.

8

THE SECRET TEACHING

Then a fan rose from her seat in the second deck above the short porch near the foul pole, put down her popcorn, put on her glove, and said this to the World-Honored One: "Lord, this game that you have made for us is excellent, profound, filled with many meanings, able to captivate the hearts of those of many worlds and many eras, the old and the young, the wise and the foolish. But Lord, this game that you have made is also boring, filled with moments of dead time more numerous than the grains of sand of all the beaches in Florida. We must endure endless trips to the mound, where pitcher and catcher place their gloves over their faces; we must endure the pitcher shaking off signs and stepping off the rubber, the batter stepping out of the box after each pitch to adjust his batting gloves; we must endure interminable replay reviews of plays we can clearly see with our own eyes. And we must endure the tedious time between innings, when at home we must stare at commercials for Viagra and beer and in the stands we must watch silly races of people dressed as hot dogs and watch ourselves doing embarrassing dances on the Jumbotron. And I will not speak of rain delays.

"I find no fault with the Blessed One. I know that everything he teaches is for the welfare of the fans, for the happiness of the fans, out of compassion for the teams, for the benefit, the welfare, and the happiness of players and fans. And so, holding a foul ball in my glove, I reverently ask the Enlightened One: Why did the Omniscient One make the game so boring?"

From right field, The Hammer spoke, saying, "Lord, outfielders are also bored as we stand waiting for the reliever to finish his warm-ups." From shortstop, the Wizard of Oz spoke, saying, "Lord, infielders are also bored as we stand on our toes, awaiting the pitch, and the pitcher shakes off the sign." From first base, Boog Powell spoke, saying, "Lord, first basemen are also bored, hoping that a batter gets hit by a pitch so that we have someone to talk to." From the bullpen, Goose Gossage spoke, saying, "Lord, relievers are also bored, sitting all game beyond the outfield fence, waiting to see if the game will be a blowout or a squeaker, waiting for the call from the pitching coach to start warming up." From the home dugout, Thurman Munson spoke, saying, "Lord, at the bottom of the inning, the players are also bored, waiting for our turn to bat only four times in a game." From the visitors' dugout, Edgar Martinez spoke, saying, "Lord, designated hitters are also bored, sitting on the bench all game, waiting to be able to bat when their spot in the lineup comes up." From the visitors' dugout, Smoky Burgess spoke, saying, "Lord, pinch hitters and backup catchers are also bored, waiting all game to see if we might have one at bat or play the field for one inning. And so, we reverently ask the Enlightened One: Why did the Omniscient One make the game so boring?"

The Buddha replied, "I made the game boring because life is also boring. I made the game like life, so that my disciples can learn to deal with boredom and to use boredom as a time to contemplate the nature of reality. Yet I also make the game boring to give my disciples, both players and fans, the time to practice the secret teaching that bestows great bliss."

Then, Ted Williams, moving to the plate, took his practice swings and said, "Long ago, the Blessed One taught me the secret teaching. By practicing the secret teaching, I batted .406 in 1941, going six for eight in the final doubleheader of the season on the road in Philadelphia. Lord, please reveal the goddamn secret teaching."

The Buddha said, "Well said, you with a lifetime OBP of .482. I now reveal the secret teaching, taught only to my most beloved disciples. It can be practiced in the dugout, it can be practiced in the on-deck circle, it can be practiced in the hotel instead of playing video games, it can be practiced in the off-season. Fans can practice it in the stands between innings and during a pitching change, they can practice it at home while watching a game with the sound muted, they can practice it in the off-season. It is the secret teaching of the bodhisattva Vajrapani, who has appeared in lifetime after lifetime, in season after season, as a professional hitter.

"For this secret teaching, one need not sit in the lotus posture. You may practice the secret teaching sitting in the stands or sitting in the dugout or sitting in the bullpen, or sitting at home in front of the television. Sit upright, with your spine straight and your shoulders level. Rest your hands in your lap, holding a baseball, your thumbs touching it at the top. Watch an inning of the game without speaking and without looking at your phone, absorbed in each pitch, just watching the action. Do not impede the baseball thoughts that arise in your mind—thoughts of what pitch should be thrown, which base to throw to, whether to take the extra base. Follow the ball as it moves around the field, from the rubber to the plate, from the bat to the warning track. Allow all baseball thoughts to flow, watching them, feeling the joy and the sorrow.

"Now, begin the main practice. In the middle of your torso, four finger breadths below your navel, imagine a tiny home plate, the size of a lentil bean, standing upright, its point pointing downward. Standing at that plate, imagine yourself as the wrathful bodhisattva of power, Vajrapani, but in the form of your favorite hitter of all time, dressed in the home uniform, to the right of the plate if right-handed, to the left of the plate if left-handed. You hold in your hand a Louisville Slugger of the finest white ash. As you take your practice swings, you point the bat upward, toward the top of your head. It is the bottom of the ninth of Game Seven of the World Series. Your team is down by a run. There are two outs and a runner is on second.

"As you sit in the posture, at the center of your chest imagine a tiny baseball, made of white horsehide with one hundred and eight red stitches, the ball the size of a mustard seed. As you step into the batter's box, concentrate all of your attention on your bat, confident that you are about to get hot, so hot that your bat begins to feel warm in your hands, as if it is ready to burst into flame. As you take your stance, the mantra 'Play ball' resounds through your mind.

"Now shift your focus to the tiny baseball in the center of your heart. It begins to descend through your body and toward the plate. Although it is a fastball, imagine it moving slowly, almost in slow motion. It is center cut, you see it well, you start your swing. As the bat strikes the ball on the sweet spot, imagine that you smell smoke. You get it all. Before running the bases, you drop your bat without flipping it and watch the ball travel toward deepest center field.

"Although the exit velocity is 120 mph, imagine the ball rising slowly, almost in slow motion. It travels straight up through your body, going beyond your navel, going beyond your heart, going completely beyond your throat, moving through your skull. As it moves upward you experience deeper and deeper feelings of joy, until the ball reaches the crown of your head, where it is caught by a child in the center field bleachers. Feel the bliss of the child, hear the roar of the crowd. Focusing on the tiny ball at the crown of your head, rest in bliss." Thus spoke the Buddha.

ENLIGHTENMENT

Then Jackie Robinson emerged from the visitors' dugout, wearing not Dodger Blue but the red and white of the Kansas City Monarchs. He came to the plate and said this to the Buddha: "World-Honored One, I was also Vajrapani, appearing first in the Negro Leagues, then on the Montreal Royals, and then on the Dodgers. In my first season in the majors, I was Vajrapani in his peaceful form, practicing the perfection of patience. In my second season, I was Vajrapani in his wrathful form, stealing second with spikes flashing. I have practiced the secret teaching for many seasons, allowing me to be an All-Star for six consecutive years, although I was already twenty-eight when I played my first major league game. Yet this secret teaching that you have revealed is a practice of heroics and home runs. In *The Baseball Sutra*, you have taught us about the impermanence of baseball, the sufferings of baseball, the emptiness of baseball. Tell us now, players and fans alike, how this wondrous game you have created teaches us how to live our lives."

The Buddha replied, "You speak the truth, you of the retired number on every team. Many thousands of players have played in the major leagues, many thousands more in the Negro Leagues and women's leagues. Then there are the minor leagues, the Little Leagues, and the softball leagues, fast pitch and slow. And this is only in this Northern Continent. In the Southern Continent and in the Eastern Continent there are so many more. Many millions around the world and across the centuries have played this game called baseball. Still, only some two hundred have achieved nirvana and entered the shrine at Cooperstown.

"Even in the major leagues, baseball is the game of the bullpen catchers, the utility infielders, the fourth outfielders, the mop-up pitchers, the journeymen, the farmhands, the September call-ups. It is the game for the casual fan and the die-hard fan. It is the game for those who suffer. I teach *The Baseball Sutra* for all players and all fans, so that they can understand the impermanence of baseball, the suffering of baseball, the emptiness of baseball, so that they can know these things and yet watch the game with contentment, that they may root for the home team, with the knowledge that if they don't win, it's a shame. So that they can take the lessons of this game into their life both on and off the field, engaging in all their deeds with insight, compassion, and non-attachment, not to retreat into the clubhouse to play poker but to take their position on the field, with their teammates, to play the game knowing full well that it will always end in loss. I teach players and fans alike to turn the game into the path.

"Wherever a father or mother plays catch with a son of good lineage or a daughter of good lineage, that place becomes a pure land. And if at the time of their death that son of good lineage or daughter of good lineage thinks of the mountain and the diamond, I will appear at their deathbed and deliver them to the diamond that is eternal, surviving the destruction that comes at the end of this degenerate age." Thus spoke the Buddha.

Rising to their feet, the managers, the coaches, the trainers, the broadcasters, the writers, the general managers, the hot dog vendors, the peanut vendors, the grounds crew, stadium security, and all the players and fans stood and cheered the words of the Buddha. So ends *The Baseball Sutra*.

ABOUT THE AUTHOR

Myra Klarman

Donald Lopez Jr. has been referred to as the only public intellectual in the field of Buddhist studies. He is the Arthur E. Link Distinguished University Professor of Buddhist and Tibetan Studies at the University of Michigan and the author, editor, and translator of many books on Buddhism, including books by His Holiness the Dalai Lama.